Many describe abortion as a "women's rights" issue, involving primarily the bodies, rights, and choices of women. However, the voices of post-abortive w̶o̶m̶... ...se who have experienced deep ... ...esult of their abortion experie... ...Serena Dyksen is filling that v... ...w she navigated her journey a... ..., a journey from a place of destruction and despair toward a future of hope and healing. Serena's story is a beautiful reminder that, even in the midst of great adversity and profound personal loss, it is possible to make beauty out of ashes, to find deep peace despite past chaos, and to exchange all-consuming sorrow for everlasting joy.

—Lia Mills
Prolife Activist, Author of *An Inconvenient Life*

With awe-inspiring vulnerability woven into every page, Serena Dyksen takes readers on a journey through a series of traumatic events in her life and the resulting revelation that there are some wounds only Christ can heal. Readers are confronted with the profound truth that the scars of abortion are real, and so are the grace and redemption of God. *She Found His Grace* is an outstanding resource for women and for anyone involved in ministry.

—Paula K. Peyton
Executive Director, Hope After Rape Conception

Serena's story is raw, riveting, and transforming as she shares heartbreaking realties and life-changing decisions that allowed her to find healing and victory through Jesus Christ. For every horrific hurt in her story, there is healing; for every tragedy, there is triumph, because she ultimately chose to accept the unconditional love of the Savior. In sharing the ugly truth about abortion and its long-lasting effects, both physically and emotionally, in her life and the life of her family, Serena is giving a voice to millions of women who have experienced the same but struggle to find a way to voice it.

—Christy Stutzman
Indiana State Representative, District 49, Middlebury/Goshen

From the very first sentence of her book, Serena drew me into the riveting story of her life and God's unfailing love for a little girl growing up in poverty. This book will bring hope and healing to those who have experienced abuse and abortion and all of us who desperately need grace and forgiveness found only at the foot of the cross. May the Lord continue to use Serena and her story to draw many to Himself, for it is only there that we are truly set free.

—Cathie Humbarger
Executive Director, Right to Life of Northeast Indiana

Everyone needs to hear Serena Dkysen's story of abortion at the hands of infamous abortionist Ulrich Klopfer—not just pro-lifers, but anyone who cares about the profound impact abortion has on women. Her story rips away the mask of "choice" and lays bare how abortion exploits women and girls and damages their psychological, physical, and spiritual health.

But Serena's story is not just a cautionary tale about the harms of abortion. It's also the moving story of how God planted seeds early in her life that would later come to flower when she hit rock bottom and finally turned to Him for help. That same grace is available to every woman who is suffering from the aftermath of abortion. This is the Good News that readers will discover in *She Found His Grace*. Read this book to really understand what's at stake in abortion—and what's possible when we trust in our loving Creator.

—Eric Scheidler
Executive Director, Pro-Life Action

SHE FOUND

HIS

Grace

SERENA DYKSEN

BRIDGE
LOGOS

Newberry, FL 32669

She Found His Grace: A True Story of Hope, Love, and Forgiveness After Abortion

Published by:
Bridge-Logos
Newberry, Florida 32669, USA
www.bridgelogos.com

Printed in the United States of America

ISBN: 978-1-61036-249-8

Library of Congress Control Number: 2020940386

Edited by Lynn Copeland

Cover by Kent Jensen | knail.com

Cover photo by Skyla Design, unsplash.com

Interior design and layout by Genesis Group

Contents

To all the women and girls who have
walked my same path of brokenness
from abortion, rape, and abuse.
Whenever a woman calls on God,
that is where
she finds his grace.
There is healing and hope!

CHAPTER ONE

The Secret

Your word is a lamp for my feet,
a light on my path.
—PSALM 119:105

It was a cold winter morning with a clear, blue sky. I was sitting on the school bus looking out the window and feeling this overwhelming emotion. With each passing house along that Indiana state road, my heart beat faster. I swallowed hard and pushed back the tears. I knew I needed help. I had to tell somebody, but I was so scared. There was always that question, *How will my parents react?* I felt overpowered by fear and shame. *How could I add more problems to my already troubled home life?*

The girl sitting next to me was two years older. She was in eighth grade, and I was in sixth. I barely knew her, but I felt I could trust her. I just blurted it out. It was the first time I told anyone what had been happening to me. I kept it a secret for so long.

Later that day as I was sitting in choir, the guidance counselor came into the classroom. She called out to the music teacher, "Can I see Serena, please?" I obediently moved forward and followed her down the long hall toward her office. She sat me down and calmly started asking me some very uncomfortable questions. I hesitated to even respond. It was one thing to tell an older student my secret, but to finally talk to an adult was even more frightening. She kept questioning me. I kept stalling. I knew the situation had gone on long enough, but how can I reveal it all?

Slowly, I began to tell her everything. As I started to answer her questions, it was like the weight of the world just lifted right off of me: the shame, the confusion, the anger. Looking back on it, I don't know how I had kept it hidden for so long.

At thirteen years old, I had no idea how to communicate what was happening to me. I barely understood it myself, but I hated it, and I just wanted it to stop. As the words rolled off my tongue, the tears streamed down my face. My uncle had been sexually abusing me, and I wanted it to end.

I don't recall the name of that eighth-grade student on the school bus that day, but I am forever grateful to her. She did the right thing in sharing my secret with an adult. If that guidance counselor had not brought me into her office that day, I don't know how long my abuse would have continued. That eighth grader rescued me. But she's just one example of how God intervened in my life to save me from further abuse and pain.

That day in the counselor's office is one critical event in the puzzle of my life. I am now slowly putting it all together and seeing the hand of God in each piece. Today, I have the advantage of seeing the bigger picture, and through every experience—good and bad—God was there all along. In his infinite grace and mercy, he was piecing it all together to complete his perfect will in my life. But to adequately tell my story, I need to share the other pieces that make up my life's puzzle.

FAMILY

I was born in 1975 in the land of Goshen—not the famous one mentioned in the Bible, but a small nondescript town in Indiana. My parents met through family connections. My father's sister married my mother's brother, and that's how my parents were introduced to each other. Both of my parents grew up in poverty: my mother in Michigan, with a large family of eleven brothers and sisters, and my father and his five siblings in Marion, Indiana. Despite their large families, there was never a strong extended family connection while I was growing up, for reasons I'd understand later.

With my sister's birth two years after me, our family of four embarked on a life constantly on the move. Before I reached age five, our little family had moved multiple times in the state of Michigan. I remember my mom, dad, sister, and me cramped in my grandparents' small camper at one point. It was one of those towable travel trailers with an oval shape. The four of us barely fit in it. It was fun for a while, through the eyes of an adventurous preschooler, but not for a normal way of living.

By the time I was in kindergarten, we had moved to a new location. There was never any consistency in how long we stayed in one place. My mother provided the steady income in the family, through various jobs in factories or nursing homes. But my father had a difficult time keeping a job. Often, I remember him coming home early from work because he was fired by his employer or decided to quit. It was a regular occurrence, which usually meant my parents couldn't pay their bills and food was scarce. There were times my mother and father packed up all we could fit in our car with barely enough room for me and my sister, and we would head out to a new home. This meant an unfamiliar school and another adjustment to strange surroundings.

My parents tried their best to find supervision for my sister and me. I remember they hired a babysitter to walk me to kindergarten and then watch my little sister during the day. My elementary school was several blocks away across a busy four-lane street with ongoing traffic. One particular morning, my babysitter left me to cross that busy street alone and to walk the rest of the way to school by myself. I was only five years old and didn't understand which roads led to my school. I got lost. A kind stranger eventually helped me to get to school that day, but unfortunately, there were several other occasions I had to find my way unsupervised.

With the constant uprooting, school was never consistent in my life and it was challenging to find some normalcy with my education. My age never aligned with the correct grade due to missing so many school days. School attendance and parental involvement weren't priorities in my family. My parents weren't the type to participate in school events, but I do remember one rare time that they came into my classroom for an open house. I had a journal on top of my school desk. The teacher had assigned the class to write in their journal each day, though mine had many blank pages because I missed so many days of school. My teacher had written the kindest note in my journal, and my mother read it out loud to me. That little personal note meant so much to me because I felt singled out and special.

Several years later, I had another teacher who showed me kindness. She would pull me aside during recess to help me with my school work. With my frequent absences, it was difficult to keep up with my assignments. That teacher always set aside a snack and chocolate milk for me while I did my school work. I think she knew I was frequently hungry and that I was one of those students who went to school without a daily breakfast. It is incredible how a little snack can mean so much to a child that it sticks out in my adult mind to this day.

Without consistent supervision, I learned at a young age that I would have to take care of myself. Our house was always filthy, and my sister and I often wore dirty clothes that smelled like cigarettes since both our parents were smokers. One day, I was incredibly proud of myself. I taught myself how to wash my clothes and set off to school wearing a freshly clean and neat outfit. But I guess I didn't understand about static cling because I was horrified when the kids at school started to laugh at me. On top of my newly cleaned clothes was an attached article of clothing. It was my underwear. I remember feeling so defeated. No matter how hard I tried to fit in, I always seemed to stick out.

Despite the poverty I grew up in—or perhaps because of it—there was always this determination in me to make things better. If I needed fresh clothes, I washed them myself. If there were no clean dishes, I would scrub the kitchen mess. One day, things were so bad that I found maggots on the dishes piled in our sink. Determined to clean every cup, plate, and piece of silverware, I rolled up my sleeves and got busy. When my mom arrived home from work, she took a dish out of the cupboard and noticed it was still dirty. She took every single item out and made me wash them all over again. That was the distinct moment that I became a people pleaser, and a lie was planted in me that I was not good enough.

There was always ongoing turmoil in my home. My father was an angry man and was physically abusive. My mother was controlling and, at times, struggled with depression. I realize now that my childhood looked very different from that of other kids at my school. Traditional family events were just not a part of my upbringing. There were no birthday parties, and I recall only a couple of holiday gatherings with extended family—one at Christmas and the other at Thanksgiving. The only family vacation we ever took was to Myrtle Beach, South Carolina, and that was a one-night stay. It was always just the four of us—just trying to get by—and rarely were we around other people or other family members. As a child, this was all I knew. It was my normal, even though it was anything but ordinary.

> I REALIZE NOW THAT MY CHILDHOOD LOOKED VERY DIFFERENT FROM THAT OF OTHER KIDS AT MY SCHOOL.

They say each generation has a choice to make, and I think this is true in my family. You only know what you know until you know better. I have watched the generational junk cycle through my family. My dad was an angry, mean man, but so was his father. My mother was emotionally and physically unstable, but she came from a family that closed each other off due to abuse and dysfunction. There reaches a point where you have to decide and choose not to continue in the same destructive family cycle. I have chosen to walk a different path which the puzzle pieces of my life will eventually reveal.

THE FARMHOUSE

There was one place we lived that was like an oasis in my childhood memories. We moved there when I was about eight years old. It sticks out in my mind for several reasons. First, it was a two-story white house on a beautiful farm in Howe, Indiana, surrounded by cornfields. The farmhouse had a wraparound porch on two sides where I would play for hours. My mother had always dreamed of having a veranda that extended around her home. She made a big deal of how special it was, and it then became special to me.

The house was set between two fields, next to a windmill that seemed to tower over the landscape. I remember the mesmerizing spin of the blades on a windy day. The farm was a wide-open playground for my sister and me to roam and explore. The irrigation trails functioned as our bike paths where we would ride for hours, occasionally stopping to play in the large silo on the property or climb the steel bars on the base of the windmill.

Inside the farmhouse was a staircase where, on any given day, my sister and I would slide down its wooden handrail for fun. But the best part of that house was that I had my very own bedroom. It was my haven. I spent hours in that room to escape the conflict in my home and avoid getting into trouble. I'd play dress-up with Avon makeup samples and listen to music. One day, my parents brought home a record player. I don't know where they got it from, but I thought it was the coolest thing ever. I played vinyl records like Hall and Oates, Toto, and Michael Jackson's *Thriller* album for hours and hours.

Despite the house being dirty and our constant family struggles, that farmhouse with the unique wraparound porch was our consistent place to live and play. It finally felt like a real home where we were able to put down roots for four years.

But what made the farmhouse such a special place was the Whistler family. Mr. Whistler was our landlord, and he was a generous and kind man. He would often stop by and give us food and gifts. There was something different about Mr. Whistler. He was a Sunday school teacher, and every Sunday he would pick up my sister and me and drive us to church. We would squeeze into the back seat of his car next to his daughter and two sons. We attended Sunday school where we would listen to a Bible lesson, and then we'd sit with the Whistler family for the church service. Mr. Whistler, his wife and kids, and even Grandpa Whistler—we would all sit together in the same row.

The highlight of my week was going to church every Sunday. It was the first time I heard about Jesus and the Bible. Occasionally I enjoyed singing in front of the whole church while making hand motions along with the lyrics. I even had the opportunity to perform in the church's Christmas play. They gave me the coveted role of Mary, which they made a big deal about. I didn't know much about the Christmas story or why it was so special. All I knew was that I was a girl who had to hold a baby doll in my arms. I remember thinking, *What's so special about the name Mary and this plastic doll?*

The Bible, Sunday school, and Jesus: It was all new to me, and I loved every minute of it. I felt such love in that church. There was also something unique about the Whistler family and the people of that congregation. I didn't understand what it was, but I gravitated toward it. It was the first time that I realized I could have something different than what was in my home. There was constant anxiety inside our walls. But every Sunday, I felt peace and comfort at church, and I wanted that kind of difference in my life.

Mr. Whistler gave me a gold-colored Good News Bible with Psalm 119:105 written on it: "Your word is a lamp for my feet, a light on my path." It was my very first Bible. Despite all the moves my family made after the farmhouse, I still have that Bible to this day. Howe, Indiana, was like a bright light on the path of my growing up years. My life would eventually take a very dark path, but God used Mr. Whistler to plant more than corn in those fields. He planted a seed in my heart that would ultimately take root.

DOWN SOUTH

Our family's next move came in the middle of the night while I was in fifth grade. My parents packed everything up again in the car, and we headed to Michigan. We left the farmhouse, my private bedroom, and the one place that gave us some stability in our lives. My mother and father dropped my sister and me off at my aunt's house, and they headed down south for North Carolina. They left us behind. I remember it was for an extended amount of time because my aunt tried to enroll us in school. The elementary school wouldn't permit us to attend because my aunt wasn't our legal guardian.

Eventually, my parents came back for us and brought us down to North Carolina. This time, our house was the newest we had ever lived in. It was located in a nice neighborhood with a school nearby. My sister was able to attend the local school, but I was bused to another elementary school on the other side of town. The district wanted to desegregate their schools, so they sent me to a school in the projects.

My bus driver went by the nickname Frog. He would either make us sit completely quiet on the bus or lead us in rap songs that had curse words. One day, we had to sit in silence. I was typically shy and didn't like to draw attention to myself. So I was horrified when he looked back and caught me whispering to another student. Not only did he yell at me, but he called me a boy. I guess he couldn't correctly identify me because I had a very short hairstyle. I wanted to crawl under the seat and hide from the embarrassment.

Living in the South was a different way of life than I'd known in the Midwest. I'll never forget the day when a student was paddled in class. A teacher spanking a student with a paddle—it was so strange to me. Then in another embarrassing moment, I made a northern-girl mistake. For an extended time, my parents would pick me up early from school. One day, the teacher asked me if this early dismissal was going to happen regularly. I answered, "I don't know." She then proceeded to scold me because I did not appropriately respond with, "I don't know, ma'am." After that day, I made sure "ma'am" was a part of my daily vocabulary.

I always felt like I stuck out as different. With this move, once again I was the new girl—from the North—in a strange school. But I was determined to fit in. I met a boy named Patrick, and I considered him my new best friend. A girl named Yolanda befriended me too. One day at recess, Yolanda mentioned that she liked a white boy who was my skin color. She asked me, "Do you like a boy?" I told her I liked Patrick, who had the same color as her skin. Suddenly, Yolanda and her friends surrounded me, and I panicked. I thought they were going to beat me up. Apparently, I wasn't allowed to like boys who looked like Patrick. White girls could not like black boys. The teacher blew the whistle to mark the end of recess, and the girls backed off. After that day, I kept to myself and stayed far away from both Yolanda and Patrick.

There seemed no point in going to school. I didn't fit in, and I was scared of the kids in my class. My parents didn't care if I went to school or stayed home. So, instead, I watched TV all day. One afternoon, a truant officer knocked on our door and began to ask my dad some questions about me. I didn't know what a truant officer was until I heard him talking to my father. "If she doesn't want to go to school, then we won't send her," was my dad's reply to the officer.

Inconsistency was just a regular part of my home life, whether it was irregular employment for my parents, unpredictable meals for our family, or my frequent absences from school. It didn't take long before we uprooted again. This time the move was more difficult for me to understand. We left our much nicer house with new furniture. My parents just packed up the car and left everything that wouldn't fit on the curb. I remember looking out the window, thinking, *Why don't we take all of those house items with us? We don't have the money for new stuff.* We took whatever could fit and left everything else behind, and headed back to Middlebury, Indiana, to a very dumpy trailer park.

NIGHTMARE

We never had much money, but going from the house in North Carolina to the trailer in Indiana was like going from riches to rags. The outside of the trailer home was a dingy white, and the inside was filthy and infested with cockroaches. My mom worked hard to get rid of all the pests. Even the trailer park neighborhood felt dirty and unsafe. My parents told us not to play with any of the other kids in the area, but I did manage to sneak out to play with two sisters and their brother. I so badly wanted to play with other children my age.

The trailer was the first time my uncle started to come around and visit with my parents. He was married to my mother's sister, and I didn't know him very well. He wasn't someone who visited us when I was younger. One day, he said to my mother that my aunt wanted to know if I would come over to their house and babysit their kids—my two younger cousins. My mom permitted me to go, and I remember being excited about babysitting and spending time with my little cousins, who were about two and four years old. I knew that babysitting was more responsibility, and at age eleven I felt proud to be asked to do an older kid's job.

One particular day, my uncle picked me up to take me to his house to babysit. Along the way, he decided to take a detour. I knew we were going the wrong direction, but he said he was taking me on a back road to teach me how to drive. I remember thinking that was a bit odd, but I hesitantly remarked, "Okay…" Then, he said, to teach me how to drive,

I needed to sit on his lap. Immediately, I knew something was not right. I felt very uncomfortable. It was an awkward situation, and I was trapped. I didn't know what to say or what to do to get out of it. He was an adult, and I was just a kid.

That was the first time he touched me inappropriately. He called it a "driving lesson," but after the lesson, all I wanted to do was get as far away from him as possible. I remember after it was over, I moved as close as I could to the passenger door, trying to hug it. He stopped at a gas station on the way to his house, and nothing was ever said.

AT THIRTEEN YEARS OLD, THIS WAS MY NIGHTMARE, AND I HAD NO IDEA HOW TO WAKE MYSELF UP FROM IT.

The next time he showed up at my house, I didn't want to go and babysit. But I didn't know how to refuse, so I got in the car with him again. Over and over, he made that detour with his vehicle, and each time I just emotionally shut down. I didn't know how to tell anyone what was happening to me. Eventually, it escalated to where he was raping me in the middle of the night in his house. At thirteen years old, this was my nightmare, and I had no idea how to wake myself up from it.

During this time, my family made another move to another trailer park. My life felt so out of control. That was when

I knew I had to tell someone. It had gone on long enough. That day on the school bus, I shared my nightmare secret with an eighth-grader.

POSITIVE

The guidance counselor called my parents into school, and I was terrified of their reaction. I was fearful of how angry they would be. I knew the tension and anxiety already in my house, and this would make things a lot worse. The counselor urged my parents to take me to see a doctor. My dad drove us to the doctor's office, and he stayed in the car while my mom and I went in. The doctor asked me all kinds of questions I couldn't answer because I didn't understand any of it. My mom responded to almost all the questions directed at me. Living in a dysfunctional home, I learned it was easier just to keep quiet and let the adults do all the talking.

The doctor examined me and gave me a pregnancy test. It came back positive. I had no idea that I was pregnant. I didn't even understand the parts of my body that would cause my pregnancy. My mother rarely talked to me about anything like that. I knew being pregnant meant having a baby, but I was clueless about what all that entailed. I don't recall being around women who were pregnant. There was so much confusion. I had finally gotten brave enough to tell someone my secret and discovered I was pregnant at thirteen years old.

The reaction of the doctor and the look on my mother's face conveyed to me that this pregnancy was not good news. That day in the doctor's office was the first time I heard the word "abortion." I had no idea what it meant, but the doctor suggested it to my mother, and she immediately responded, "Yes, that's what we are going to do."

CHAPTER TWO

Women's Pavilion

*"For I know the plans I have for you," declares
the Lord, "plans to prosper you and not to
harm you, plans to give you hope and a future."*
—JEREMIAH 29:11

My scheduled appointment was at the Women's Pavilion
Center in South Bend, Indiana. My family doctor
warned my mother about the protesters who would be outside. "As soon as you arrive, get out of the car and walk into
the clinic very quickly," he cautioned. "Those people hate
you. They will be yelling and harassing both of you."

I watched my mother's reaction. "If they come near me,
I'll knock them out. It's none of their damn business!" she
remarked in anger.

I was bound by fear and anxiety. The brief moment of
freedom I experienced after revealing my sexual abuse was
quickly swept away by the revelation that I was pregnant. As
a thirteen-year-old, I don't know how I was able to carry that
weight of emotion. The chaos in my home intensified, and I

feared the upcoming day of my scheduled abortion. *Would protestors be yelling at us?* I wondered. *What will my parents do if confronted by angry people at the clinic?* And the persistent question in my head was, *What exactly is abortion?*

WOMEN'S PAVILION

The history surrounding the Women's Pavilion drew controversy even before it opened its doors in 1978. Its first location was on St. Louis Street, near St. Joseph's Hospital. The hospital filed an injunction against the abortion facility claiming it would cause St. Joseph's "irreparable damages"[1] by the community associating it with the nearby abortion services. The leaders of the Catholic hospital opposed abortion.

During this time, various pro-life organizations stood outside the clinic, some with protest signs and anti-abortion chants. There were sit-in demonstrations that created a hostile environment with protesters screaming and yelling at those entering the clinic. The St. Joseph County Right to Life organization was also a prominent presence in the area with many members standing outside the abortion facility. They were often lumped among the "haters" but they had a very different mission.

The Right to Life's mission statement is "to protect and defend the most fundamental right of humankind, the right to life of every innocent human being from the beginning of life to natural death."[2] Their presence outside the Women's Pavilion is to provide what they term "sidewalk counseling." No angry chants or violent protests. Their counselors were there to love and support women—even young teens like me —to offer an alternative to abortion with resources to protect motherhood and life. Years later, as an adult, I would come to understand the phrase "every innocent human being" and the Right to Life's purpose to protect the sanctity of human life. I would also stand side-by-side with those connected with that organization. But on that day in 1989, I didn't know about Right to Life or any pro-life organization. All I knew was that I had an appointment at an abortion clinic, and there would be people outside who hated me.

My parents drove to the clinic's new location at 2010 Ironwood Circle. As soon as we arrived, we noticed there wasn't a single person standing outside. Pro-life groups regularly stood behind a chain-link fence bordering the parking lot, but on this particular day, all was quiet. My mom mentioned to my father, "I am glad those people aren't here."

THEIR COUNSELORS WERE THERE TO LOVE AND SUPPORT WOMEN— EVEN YOUNG TEENS LIKE ME.

The building had an angled roof with an overhang that led to the front entrance. We walked into the clinic, and I noticed just one lady with short brown hair sitting in the waiting area. When they called my name, I was led down a hall to a counselor's room without my parents. I quickly noticed a difference between this medical facility and my family doctor's office. *This place is dirty,* I thought to myself. The counselor began to talk to me.

I didn't understand anything she was explaining, but I do remember her describing that the doctor would remove a clump of cells from me. I felt so overwhelmed and scared. I had to trust the fact that my doctor, my parents, and all the adults involved in this decision had my best interests in mind. The counselor asked if I was ready for the abortion, and I nodded my head apprehensively.

I was ushered into another room, where someone told me to take off my clothes and put on a medical gown. A nurse directed me to lie on a table, and she guided my feet into stirrups. I was uncomfortable and embarrassed. I was so unsure about what was going to happen to me. As I was waiting on the table, a middle-aged white man with gray hair walked in. He smiled at me and said, "This won't take very long."

All of a sudden, a blaring vacuuming sound began. I'll never forget it. It was a disturbing suction noise much louder than any vacuum cleaner at home. I then experienced the most excruciating pain I had ever felt. I screamed in agony. The only way to describe it was a violent jolt against my whole body. The pain was unbearable, and I cried out again. The abortion doctor looked at me and angrily shouted, "Shut up!" A nurse came by my side and held my hand to quiet me down. I was in total shock over what just took place. I'll never forget the intensity of that pain and the way the doctor callously yelled at me.

Once the procedure was over, I was led to a recovery room with a few other women. We all sat in brown recliners, but no one made eye contact. I felt frail and exhausted and was reeling from the pain. The shock of what just happened left me dazed and confused. After some time, the nurse came back to walk me out to my parents in the waiting area. As soon as I stood up, a gush of blood poured out of me. I began hemorrhaging. The nurse never called the doctor back to check on me. They just hurried me out of the clinic. I was so weak I could barely walk. My dad picked me up, pulled me over his shoulder, and carried me out to the car. I didn't go back for a follow-up visit, and I never entered that clinic again.

Many years later, I found my mother's journal, where she wrote about that horrific day. She heard my screams out in the waiting room, but the staff would not allow her to come back with me. I often wondered whether my parents would comprehend the violence and trauma I experienced that day if they had been allowed into the abortion room. But I realize now that my parents were just as ignorant about the procedure of abortion as I was. They were directed by our family doctor, whom they trusted.

I will never be able to erase the memory of that day and that unbearable pain. I have yet to experience anything like that in my adult life. Which makes me wonder, did the staff at that clinic administer any pain medication during my abortion procedure? It didn't feel like it. All I know for sure was that my abortion was the second act of violence done to me beyond my control.

GUILTY

On February 21, 1989, my abuser pleaded guilty to a crime of sexual assault in the third degree. According to court records, he denied molesting me in the car, but he admitted raping me on two occasions in his home. He stated in the court record, "I got a feeling to have sex with her." The judge's sentencing said, "There has been extreme suffering, and I refer to the anguish of the victim's family and the victim, as reported in the victim's impact statement by the parents and the remarks by Mr. [abuser's name]. Secondly, the incredible experience on the child having to undergo the abortion, not only the physical but mental, and emotional experience."[3]

At twenty-five years old, a married father of two young children, my uncle was sentenced to seven to fifteen years of incarceration. His mental health test noted that he had a personality profile of a regressed pedophile. It also stated that he had sexual activity with cousins and relatives, yet his lawyer commented that he was a "salvageable" pedophile.

> **GOD'S MERCY THAT HAS BEEN GIVEN TO ME IS THE SAME MERCY THAT CAN BE EXTENDED TO MY ABUSER.**

At the time, I was unaware of all the details surrounding his arrest and sentencing. My parents shielded me from all of it, probably realizing I had suffered enough trauma already. I do remember walking into the courthouse and having to enter a courtroom and stand before a judge. He asked me to state my name, age, and grade. I did, and then I immediately walked right back out. That was my only experience with the court case and my abuser's sentencing.

My mother wrote a letter that was included in the presentation report that was read by the sentencing judge:

> I had to take my little girl for [an] abortion on Valentine's day, I had to set in the lobby and hear her beg and scream and cry for me to help her and I couldn't, as much as I wanted to take her pain and hurt from her I couldn't, all I could do was cry and pray to [G]od that she made it threw this o.k. I know my little girl and what impact this has done on her, I see the hurt, the shame, the guilt of thinking it must be her fault and the humiliation of it, her little eyes are not the same at all, they look dead. The shine that used to melt your heart away is gone now and it all but kills me to see that.[4]

Many years later, I came face to face with the graphic details and written testimonies on those court records. The record revealed that when I learned that my little sister was to spend the night at my uncle's house, I stayed overnight as well to protect her. That was one of the nights he raped me.

I didn't realize all the turmoil my family went through and my mother's heartache over what had happened to me. The fact that my abortion took place on Valentine's Day was also something that I did not know until my adult healing journey. My abuser took so much from my family and me. And yet, God's mercy that has been given to me is the same mercy that can be extended to my abuser.

The judge remarked in the court records:

> If she, Serena, is extremely lucky, with continued strong family support, competent therapy, and personal determination, we can certainly hope that she'll

regain much of that self-esteem. But she's going to be missing a major portion of it through the next five or ten years as she addresses the most important questions of her life; the continuation of her education and finding a mate.[5]

As I read those remarks by the judge, I realized he had no idea the path my life would take. I was a young girl with my whole future ahead of me, but the judge knew the obstacles I would face.

I know that God allowed certain puzzle pieces of my sexual abuse and abortion to be hidden or blocked out. Some memories I repressed and others were uncovered as an adult when I read the court transcript. The passing of time does heal emotional wounds, but I also believe God's merciful hand is a part of the timing process. God would reveal my trauma when I was ready to begin my healing journey.

MIDDLE SCHOOL

I don't remember much about those days, weeks, or even months after my abortion. I had emotionally shut it all away. My parents never mentioned it again, and life went on as if it never happened. But there was a definite shift in my personality, and by seventh grade, I began to struggle with depression. I lost all resilience that characterized me as a child. Social activities were no longer fun. The one activity my parents often allowed me to do on weekends was to go to the roller skating rink. I remember being asked to go and having no desire to skate with my friends. I could feel myself shutting down and becoming increasingly unhappy, but I didn't understand why.

During the eighth grade, we moved again to a new trailer park in the area. This home was slightly cleaner than the previous one. It was while we lived here that I started to sneak out in the middle of the night to hang out with some older kids. I began drinking and smoking and trying my best to fit into what I thought was the popular crowd.

Around this time, I began to notice a change in my mother. She started having physical health problems as well as mental issues like depression. My home life was always chaotic, but the difference in her was disturbing. She was becoming emotionally unstable, and her behavior was unpredictable. At one point, she had a nervous breakdown.

While chaos continued at home, I spent more time with friends. By age fourteen, I started dating a boy who was well-liked in the group. I remember thinking, *If he likes me, then I'll finally feel special and worth something.* He showed interest in me, and it wasn't long before we started having sex. There was fear surrounding my decision to sleep with him, but my need to feel accepted and loved convinced me that I shouldn't say no. We didn't use contraception, and pregnancy never crossed my mind. I just wanted someone to care about me. Of course, at the time, I had no idea that there were other girls he was sleeping with besides me.

With my bouts of depression, I also began to feel increasingly angry. I hated my parents and wanted to run away. I dreamed of packing up my things and getting as far away from them as possible. I wanted a better life, and I thought they were so screwed up. It never occurred to me that any of these feelings—my depression, my rebellion, or my anger—were side effects of my abortion. It would be years before I would make that connection. All I knew was that I was angry inside.

Today, as I look back on my abortion and those early teen years, I treasure God's Word in Psalm 139:13–16:

> For you created my inmost being; you knit me together in my mother's womb. I praise you because I am fearfully and wonderfully made; your works are wonderful, I know that full well. My frame was not hidden from you when I was made in the secret place, when I was woven together in the depths of the earth. Your eyes saw my unformed body; all the days ordained for me were written in your book before one of them came to be.

In those darkest moments of my life, I know that God was with me all along. He reminds me, *Serena, I knitted you in your mother's womb. Bad things were going to come, but I declared I have a plan to prosper you and not to harm you. I not only say it, but I declare it.* I can live and breathe this out now because my life took a path toward healing. But as I relive this time in my memory, there is no doubt that the choice that was made for me at age thirteen slowly began to destroy my family and me.

CHAPTER THREE

Little Girl

"You intended to harm me, but God intended it for good to accomplish what is now being done, the saving of many lives."
—GENESIS 50:20

My family moved once again. I lost count at this point of how many places we lived. We left the trailer park and relocated to an older home in the country. Fortunately, it was in the same school district, and I was about to start my freshman year of high school. The night before school started, I was allowed to invite my friend Jenny over for a sleepover. This was a rare occurrence and a treat to have a friend stay the night.

Jenny and I got on the school bus the next morning and sat together, excited about starting our first day of high school. The bus made a stop several miles down the road in front of a brown house, and four boys loaded on and headed toward the back. I immediately noticed one of the boys wearing a jean jacket and thought to myself, *He is cute!* It would be weeks before I would talk to that boy, but I took notice of him every morning as he got on the bus.

BRUCE

One day the jean-jacket boy was sitting in the back of the bus, and he made a tongue-in-cheek comment loud enough for all the girls to hear. "No girls are allowed to sit in the back of the bus," he proudly stated. That ridiculous comment gave me boldness to approach him. "Can I sit with you?" I flirted and teased. He slid over, and I sat beside him. His name was Bruce Dyksen, and he was a high school junior. From that day forward, we sat together on the bus.

Bruce doesn't recall that silly comment he made, but he does recall me approaching him: "She was outgoing, social, and I remember thinking, *Now there's a girl I would like to know better.* A couple of weeks went by with our casual bus conversations and flirtation, until Bruce finally got up the nerve to ask me on a date. I said yes, but I told him he would have to ask my parents first.

On our first date, Bruce showed up at my house driving a gray Ford van. He took me to Dairy Queen, mini-golf, and then to a park in Middlebury, a nearby town. From that very first date, we began to hang out regularly. He asked me to the prom, and we went along with another couple. The tradition was to attend the prom on Saturday and the after-prom on Sunday. We traveled to Cedar Point Amusement Park in Ohio on Sunday, and it was a fun weekend for all of us.

We spent more and more time together with just the two of us, without much accountability or supervision. Soon we started having sex and, like many teenagers, rarely thought about the consequences of having a sexual relationship. For me, my upbringing seemed to contribute to my poor decision-making and continual bad choices. But for Bruce, he grew up in a different home environment. He came from a Christian family and a stable home life as the oldest of four boys. Bruce knew as a Christian that sex outside marriage was wrong but didn't give it much thought.

Right from the beginning of our relationship, my parents did not like Bruce. My mom was very vocal about how she disliked him and thought he was very controlling. If Bruce came around the house, it caused conflict and tension. Bruce noticed right away the difference in my family compared to his own. He watched as my dad was in and out of work, unable to keep a stable job. He witnessed the continual dysfunction and the arguing over little things that didn't matter. One day, Bruce even stood up to my dad for treating me poorly. It's a wonder Bruce continued to date me, having to deal with my family. I often think back to that time and give him a lot of credit. Bless his heart for sticking around.

"NO WAY!"

By June, at the end of my freshman year, and at the end of Bruce's junior year, we were still dating and spending all of our time together. We also kept having sex but were now using contraception—until one day when we made a choice not to use protection. It wasn't long before I had my suspicions that I might be pregnant. I told Bruce, and we decided to go somewhere out of the area to take a pregnancy test. We made an appointment for a pregnancy test at Planned Parenthood in Elkhart, Indiana. At the time, I was working part-time at a gas station. I called my boss and told him I wouldn't be in that day.

Bruce drove me to the appointment, and we had a difficult time finding the building. It was in a bad part of town that we were not familiar with. We had no idea what we were doing or where we were going, but we knew we were in trouble and needed help. I remember Planned Parenthood was located inside an old school building and surrounded by the housing projects in Elkhart. As Bruce and I walked into the building, we both felt very nervous over our possible situation. The only question running in both of our minds was, *Are we pregnant?*

WE WERE JUST TWO TEENAGE KIDS—TENTH AND TWELFTH GRADERS—AND WE WERE MONTHS AWAY FROM HAVING A BABY.

I took a pregnancy test... and the results came back positive. Bruce and I walked out of the building both completely stunned. We sat in Bruce's car in the parking lot of Planned Parenthood and tried to figure out what we should do. That's when Bruce asked me, "What do you think about abortion?" That word was like a powerful trigger and memories I had pushed down and blocked from surfacing began flooding my mind. It was like my brain was on a fast rewind. My rape, the positive pregnancy test, my parents, the abortion clinic, the memory of that horrific pain—"No, absolutely not! I will not have an abortion!" I emphatically declared.

"I don't know why I mentioned the word abortion," Bruce recalls. He doesn't remember if they said something in Planned Parenthood or if he picked up literature, but he knew abortion was an option when you found yourself pregnant. "I was really naïve about abortion. I didn't understand it, and I wasn't exposed to any pro-abortion activism, or pro-life activism either," Bruce acknowledged. "It was the early 1990s, and there wasn't much news about abortion, and it wasn't something we talked about at home or mentioned in church."

Bruce had no idea I would react so harshly to that word or why—so sitting there in the car, I proceeded to share my abortion story.

He listened as I revealed my rape and how my parents took me to get an abortion when I was just thirteen. I left out details about my sexual abuse, but I did tell him about the traumatic experience in the abortion clinic. I was passionate about my objection to abortion. I repeated with determination, "No way!" Bruce got very quiet and hesitated before responding. There was silence between us, and then he softly replied, "Okay, we will not do that."

HAVING A BABY

The two of us made the most crucial decision of our lives that day. We agreed we would have this baby together. We also made conscious decisions that we never shared at the time. I determined to have the baby even if he wouldn't support me. Bruce made up his mind, too. "I committed to supporting her, no matter what happened in our future," he recalls. We were just two teenage kids—tenth and twelfth graders—and we were months away from having a baby.

Ironically, we would make that decision together outside the walls of Planned Parenthood, the largest abortion provider in the country. That particular Planned Parenthood referred people elsewhere for abortions. I realize now that I might have been referred to the Women's Pavilion in South Bend, where my abortion took place. There was no way I was going to step through those doors ever again.

While we were gone for the appointment, my boss called my mother. The two of them were friends, and he was worried about me because it was unusual for me to take off from work. My mother questioned me about where I was but I made up an excuse for my absence. However, I felt I needed to tell my boss the truth but asked him not to say anything to my mom. A few of our friends and my boss were the only ones who knew I was pregnant. I had no idea how to break the news to my parents, so I kept it a secret from them for several weeks.

One morning my mother came into my bedroom and woke me up. "Serena, are you pregnant?" she asked. I simply responded, "Yup." She looked at me and then immediately walked right back out. My mother had discovered I was pregnant by snooping in my room and finding a note I had written to Bruce. My parents were furious with me. "You and Bruce need to go and tell his parents," they both urged. Bruce and I set up a time to meet with his mom and dad. We were scared to tell them our news.

Together we sat on the couch in the Dyksen family's living room, and his parents sat across from us on two recliners. I felt the nervousness in the room. Bruce stalled the conversation several times. How do you tell your parents that as you're about to enter your last year of high school, you are also going to enter fatherhood? It was not an easy conversation to have. Finally, Bruce spoke up and told them, "Serena is pregnant!" Their facial expressions revealed their shock. I remember looking up at them, and all I could say was, "I am really, really sorry!"

Bruce's mother and father responded with so much love for both of us. I could tell they were stunned by our news, but they both put their arms around us and loved us in that very difficult moment. I knew what Bruce and I did was wrong, but his parents showed grace and mercy to us. But they did strongly urge us that we had to stop having sex. Bruce's dad called his other three sons into the room and told them our news. He wanted Bruce's brothers to be aware of the situation so that they could also deal with the conversations that would ultimately be shared at school.

The Dyksen family's pastor came over to the house and counseled all of us together. "Our pastor told my parents that it was important that we get in front of this situation and talk to people honestly about what was happening," Bruce recalled. "It was a stressful time in my home, but my parents reached out to their church, and in turn, the church reached out and supported both me and Serena."

THE PROPOSAL

It was clear from that first day when we decided we would have the baby that Bruce was committed to me. The summer before his senior year, he decided to try out for soccer. It was a busy summer for him as he juggled his work at McDonald's with his training to qualify for the soccer team. He would run the three-mile distance from his house to mine and stop to say hello on his training runs. Eventually, his coach told him that he needed to choose between his job at McDonald's and soccer. Bruce decided to work. "I knew that my job and making money was important with Serena being pregnant," Bruce recalls.

His decision to keep his job made me realize that Bruce was a gift from God in my life. He was only seventeen years old, but he was already working and supporting our baby and me. Bruce looks back at that time a little differently. "I just put my head down and was focused on what I needed to do," Bruce said. "I never really stopped to evaluate how I felt about the situation. I just moved forward and took care of what needed to be done."

One day while I was working at the gas station, Bruce stopped by for a surprise visit. All of a sudden he pulled out a ring and right then and there he asked me to marry him. I don't know which was more of a shock: the fact that he asked me or that he decided to "pop the question" at a gas station of all places. We laugh about it now. He proposed to me, and I said yes. He left, and I went back to work. "The only thing missing was a bag of chips and a hot dog," Bruce jokingly remarks about the proposal scenario.

TEEN PREGNANCY

At the beginning of high school, I was 4'10" in height and about 97 pounds. I was very tiny. By the beginning of my sophomore year, I started classes with my ever-growing belly. School was still a constant struggle for me like it had been all along, but I kept plugging away. I was determined to graduate high school even if I was pregnant. It was challenging being pregnant as a student. Most people were supportive of me, and I had several close girlfriends I could depend on, and they even threw me a baby shower. My math teacher, however, was not so supportive. He knew I was pregnant but would not allow me to use the restroom during class. One day, I had to go so badly, but he refused to let me leave. I thought I was going to wet my pants. After that, I got a doctor's note so that I could use the bathroom when I needed to in school.

Things got worse at home during my pregnancy. There was continual fighting and yelling, and my mother's controlling issues increased. She did not like Bruce and tried to push him out of my life. I constantly fought with my mother, usually over her not allowing me to see Bruce. My father was often mean and angry, and one day his physical abuse got so bad that I ran away from home. Bruce's parents let me stay the night at their house just to keep me safe from his rage.

I didn't feel much support from my parents during my pregnancy. I remember just wanting some type of normalcy in my home, and this caused more tension with my parents. I felt like a grown-up at this point with all that had happened in my life. Being pregnant while working and attending school was extremely difficult. I remember looking forward to going to school just to get away from all the stress in my family and to spend time with Bruce. There was no foundation at home that made me feel supported, but that was the nature of the family I came from.

Bruce's family was very different from mine. They had the support of the church to help them in their time of need. My family did not go to church. As Christians, Bruce's parents knew the love of Jesus Christ, which allowed them to offer grace and love to us in our time of need. I witnessed their firm and loving commitment to the two of us despite our poor decisions. Through little things, like their family praying before we started a meal, they pointed to their need for God in their lives. My parents never experienced the love of God, and they didn't know how to love me properly in return. I was in the middle of two family extremes. I knew the factor that made all the difference was faith in God. I gravitated toward that kind of love. It was the same love that Mr. Whistler had shown my family when we lived in the farmhouse. Once again, it was the church and now Bruce's Christian family where I felt a sense of belonging and acceptance.

THE CHURCH

The one place where Bruce and I felt genuinely supported during my pregnancy was at his church, Greene Road Christian Reformed. That congregation loved on both of us from the very start. We never felt judged, and they pointed us to the Word of God and Jesus Christ for our salvation. There I was, pregnant at sixteen, and the people there welcomed me with open arms. The church provided for us in so many ways. A couple who were youth leaders in the church—who had a similar experience of getting pregnant out of wedlock—mentored the two of us. The congregation even gave us a baby shower to help with all our baby needs. If the church had not helped us, I honestly don't know what our lives would look like today.

I have to laugh at the scenario of my church experience. When my family lived in the farmhouse in Howe, Indiana, and Mr. Whistler took me to his church, I was chosen to play the role of Mary in the Christmas program. There I was holding a baby doll in my arms and wondering, *What is the big deal about this baby?* While my lack of understanding of the Bible made that role in the Christmas play insignificant to me, it speaks volumes to me today. The pregnant teenager named Mary carried the Savior of the world. My Savior and my Redeemer. But there's a common thread shared between us. She knew the burden of being a pregnant, unwed teenager. And although there was no sin with Mary's pregnancy, there was redemption. That redemption came through the birth of her Baby, Jesus Christ. I am so glad I now understand that the gift of that Baby—the Son of God—brings salvation. God would continually reveal to me his redemption plan for my life, and I know it started with that precious life growing inside of me.

CASSIE NICOLE

I was at home on Sunday, March 14, 1993, and my mother was convinced I was going to have the baby that night. "Call Bruce and tell him to come over," she told me. I had been having Braxton Hicks contractions (false labor) all week long, so I didn't give my situation much thought. I figured the uncomfortable feelings I was experiencing were simply more of the same, and if I went to the hospital, they would just send me back home. Bruce came over after church, and we hung out together on a lazy Sunday afternoon. At 9:30 that evening, my mom said we needed to go to the hospital. I thought it was a waste of time but agreed to go.

When we arrived at the hospital, the staff checked me and found I was 8 centimeters dilated. I had no clue I was so close to having the baby. As I was prepped for delivery, I remember the nurse saying to me, "You can scream if you need to; you are about to have this baby!" I told her I was okay and that I didn't feel much pain. At 11:17 p.m., without requiring any pain medication, I gave birth to a healthy baby girl. I was blessed with an uncomplicated pregnancy and quick delivery.

When Bruce and I saw her, we cried tears of joy. Cassie Nicole was 6 pounds and 11 ounces, with blue eyes and peach fuzz hair. She was healthy and perfect. There was so much joy that evening in the hospital room. All the stress and tension with my parents was overshadowed by the birth of our beautiful baby girl. I could see the excitement in my mother's and father's eyes. Bruce's parents and brothers arrived the next day and were overjoyed as they each took turns holding Cassie. Bruce's dad was especially proud. He finally got the little girl he had always wanted through the gift of his first granddaughter. This little girl was already blessing both families on day one.

> LIFE MAY NOT GO AS PLANNED, BUT GOD GAVE US THIS BEAUTIFUL GIFT NAMED CASSIE NICOLE.

Bruce and I were excited to be parents, but we knew the tremendous challenges that lay ahead of us. He was about to graduate high school, and I had to figure out how to finish my sophomore year and raise a baby as a high school student. We were nervous and scared about not messing it all up. But as soon as you hold your baby in your arms that first time, there's a quiet reassurance that everything is going to be okay. Life may not go as planned, but God gave us this beautiful gift named Cassie Nicole.

At the time of my pregnancy, we never told Bruce's family that we discussed abortion. It was only recently that we began to share all the details surrounding Cassie's birth. In 2019 when one of Bruce's brothers heard my story, he wrote the following:

> I'm so heartbroken by what you had to endure, and in the same breath, I am so glad God took what was meant for evil to produce so much good. I nearly wept reading about Cassie's birth story. Oh, Lord, thank you for convincing Serena to speak up and say NO! For sparing Cassie's life! For filling Bruce with the courage to come alongside Serena and never leave her. Serena, thank you for saying YES to life!

As I relive those days in my mind, I know that the enemy intended to destroy me. Over the years, my abortion would take so much from me, but it didn't take the life of our daughter, Cassie. It saved her. Whatever evil was meant for me, "God meant it for good" (Genesis 50:20). God brought beauty from tragedy. The day Cassie was born, I made a commitment to her. She would have a different life than I had, and she would know that she was well loved.

CHAPTER FOUR

Young Love

*Love does not delight in evil but rejoices with the
truth. It always protects, always trusts, always
hopes, always perseveres. Love never fails.*
—1 CORINTHIANS 13:6–8

We may have been young and naïve about parenting,
but we loved our little girl and were excited about
being new parents. Unfortunately, we didn't have the typical
parenting experience of bringing our new baby home from
the hospital as a couple. I brought Cassie home with my
family, and Bruce had just a few months of his senior year to
concentrate on before his graduation. Reality quickly settled
in, and life became pretty chaotic.

EMANCIPATION

I was living at home trying to figure out how to be a teenage
mom, all while struggling to finish my sophomore year of
high school. Of course, with a baby to take care of when I got
home from school, I was no longer working at the gas station.

On top of all that, my parents were making it difficult for Bruce and his family to spend time with Cassie. My mother for some reason was determined to get Bruce out of my life. There was constant friction between both families. Bruce's dad rarely argued with anyone, but I remember seeing him confront my father when he came over to visit his grand-daughter. My dad told him he couldn't see Cassie and they argued. He finally got to see her through the front door but was unable to hold her. The stress in my house was over-whelming. As much as possible, I stayed out of the ongoing tension between our parents. Caring for a newborn was all I could handle.

I was very protective of Cassie in my house because of my parents' erratic behavior and constant control. I recall letting my dad watch Cassie only one time when I was at a breaking point and needed some sleep. But it was only once. My home life was just not the kind of environment where I felt I could let my parents help with caring for Cassie. Even-tually, things escalated to where I knew the best solution for all of us was to move out of the house.

Chuck and Barbara Taylor, friends of Bruce's parents, graciously offered a room where Cassie and I could stay. I packed up all of our things, and my parents drove Cassie and me out to the Taylors' home. It was a bed and breakfast located in a log cabin in the woods, down a long wooded lane. It was a quiet, stress-free place, and I was thankful for their generosity. They allowed me to stay with Cassie as long as I needed—rent-free!

As a way to thank the Taylors for allowing me to live in their house, I tried to help out with various tasks. But I al-ways felt awkward like I was in their way. I spent a lot of time alone in my room with Cassie. Chuck and Barbara never made me feel out of place, but my insecurity always got the best of me. I felt like a fish out of water. There I was living on my own at seventeen years old with a newborn, and I was always worried about how I measured up. It was the beginning of what I now call "pulling from my root system." The years of living in constant dysfunction were affecting me and my self-confidence.

My relationship with Bruce was also becoming difficult. He was a good father and very hands-on from the beginning, but as new parents, we had to learn how to relate to each other. It was challenging not to be able to parent together under the same roof. We also tried to keep up some form of a dating relationship. He would visit me at the Taylors' house, but we often ended up arguing. There were so many new responsibilities to deal with, and my insecurity became a big problem in our relationship. I tended to deal with our difficulties by arguing because I mimicked what I knew from watching my parents. There was an unhealthy pattern developing in our relationship.

On top of everything, there was still tension with my parents. Moving out of the house was the right decision, but I soon realized that I needed to break away entirely from my parents' control. I filed for emancipation to sever all legal ties with them so I could marry before age eighteen. Bruce and I were going to get married, and it was better to do it sooner than later. "We were trying to be proactive," Bruce recalls, "because things were not moving in the right direction."

I arrived at the courthouse and had to provide documents that I was financially secure to break away from my parents. I had to list my housing and show I was able to provide for my daughter and myself. I listed Bruce's financial contribution on the documents. I was only about six months away from turning eighteen, but I couldn't wait any longer. We knew we had to resolve this issue with my family. Bruce and I wanted to get married and parent Cassie together as a family.

GRADUATION AND WEDDING DAY

It was Bruce's idea to have our wedding on the same day as his high school graduation. All of his family—including both sets of grandparents—would already be in town for his graduation ceremony. Why not add a wedding to the mix? We both laugh at the decision now, but I wouldn't suggest scheduling two major life events in one day.

On the morning of June 5, 1993, I had to get up very early to be at the church. Our wedding ceremony was at ten o'clock in the morning. I planned to get to the church before Bruce. I didn't want him to see me until I walked down the aisle. When I arrived at the church, he was already there dressed and ready to go. I was so annoyed that he got there first. I hurried to get ready the best I could. It was a flurry of activity, and by the time ten o'clock arrived, I barely felt ready.

Up to the day of my wedding, I didn't know if my family would even show up. My parents said they didn't want to come because they didn't have nice clothes to wear. I had mixed feelings about them coming. It had only been about three months since Cassie had been born, but so much had happened during that short time. I became a new mom, moved out of my house, filed for emancipation from my parents, struggled to finish my sophomore year of school, and planned a wedding. It was a stressful time in all of our lives, but Bruce and I knew we were making the right decision by getting married.

When I saw my parents at the church, I was relieved. I am not sure where they got their clothes, but they were appropriately dressed for a wedding. Someone even provided a dress for my sister to wear as well. I choked back tears when I saw my dad. He was wearing a black suit with a pink striped tie that matched the pink flowers in my wedding bouquet. It was the first time I had ever seen my dad dressed in a suit. It is still so difficult to describe my emotions that day with him by my side. I had been through so much turmoil with my family. But on that day, my father was there to walk me down the aisle. He held my arm with a proud smile on his face, and happy tears filled my eyes. It was a special moment for both of us.

We managed to pull off the wedding with the help of Bruce's family, our friends, and the congregation of Greene Road Christian Reformed Church. I had two bridesmaids, and Bruce had two groomsmen. Our wedding reception was held in the basement of the church building where we served cake and punch. We even decorated the reception area with old prom decorations from our high school. We were broke teenagers, so anything cheap was welcomed to help spruce up the place.

During the reception, Bruce's best man had to leave because he was scheduled to work at McDonald's that day. He left before it was time to give the best man's speech, so Bruce's friend Chuck stepped in and provided the speech unprepared. We laugh about this now. We don't know why his best man didn't decide to take the day off of work or at least go in later, but then again, we were all a bunch of naïve teenagers at a wedding ceremony that day.

Following the reception, our parents, relatives, and some people from the church helped us move into our new apartment that afternoon. We had found an apartment complex offering low-income housing, which we were able to afford on Bruce's income from McDonald's. They unpacked boxes and helped us set up our new home. People in the church donated some of their furniture including a huge box television set. We were even gifted with a waterbed mattress, and Bruce made a wooden frame to fit around it. Nothing matched but we were very thankful for all the help and everyone's kindness to us. By late afternoon, we were all moved in and I was exhausted. It had already been a very long day. All I wanted to do was take a long nap, but we still had Bruce's graduation to attend that evening.

> IT WAS THE MOST CRUCIAL DECISION OF OUR LIVES. IT WAS IN THE PARKING LOT OF PLANNED PARENTHOOD THAT WE CHOSE LIFE.

Once we were primarily moved in, we got ready for Bruce's ceremony at seven o'clock. I sat in the audience, holding our three-month-old daughter on my lap. We watched as her dad—my new husband of only a few hours—received his high school diploma. It was a full day surrounded by our family and friends with lots of joy and emotions.

Bruce's grandparents were able to attend both the wedding and his graduation. "My grandfather—on my dad's side —put fifty dollars in my hand and gave me some encouraging advice," recalls Bruce. "I rarely saw my grandfather get emotional. He and my grandmother had some very difficult times in their marriage that God helped them through, and he wanted to show their support and encourage me."

There is no way to accurately convey how grateful we were for all the love and support we were given during that time in our lives. It is no coincidence that we chose Scripture verses about love to be read at our wedding:

> Love is patient, love is kind. It does not envy, it does not boast, it is not proud. It does not dishonor others, it is not self-seeking, it is not easily angered, it keeps no record of wrongs. Love does not delight in evil but rejoices with the truth. It always protects, always trusts, always hopes, always perseveres. Love never fails. (1 Corinthians 13:4–8)

On our wedding day, we certainly didn't know the future of our marriage. But we did decide something as a couple almost a year before that day. It was the most crucial decision of our lives. It was in the parking lot of Planned Parenthood that we chose life, and God revealed to us through that decision that "love never fails."

There was ongoing chaos, but there was also joy, and that joy stemmed from that beautiful baby God gave to us. Yes, we were very young and not only new parents but newly married. We realized our situation wasn't ideal, especially by society's standards. Bruce had the advantage of being a high school graduate, but I had two more years of school to go. None of the events in our lives could have been predicted. We didn't plan it this way, but God took our unplanned pregnancy and created a family out of it. "Now, as I look back, I realize God had been taking care of us the whole time," Bruce recalls. "I might have doubted how we would manage to have a baby as teenagers, but God had our lives in his hands."

MARRIED LIFE

Our church had collected some money so that we could stay at a hotel in Goshen on our wedding night. Someone offered to watch Cassie that evening, and Bruce and I had one night away for our honeymoon. The next day, we picked Cassie up and started our lives as married teen parents in our small one-bedroom apartment in Middlebury.

After graduation, Bruce started working for his dad's business in home remodeling and construction. I enjoyed staying home with Cassie that summer before my junior year of high school. We eventually met another couple in the area who paid me to babysit their kids and occasionally let me do our laundry at their place. Stacy and Eric were older than us and helped us out as new parents. It was nice to have friends living nearby. They were kind to us and would watch Cassie if I needed extra help or had to run errands.

We settled into our life as a family of three. When I returned to school in the fall, Cassie was cared for during the day by an Amish family in the area. They were friends of Bruce's family, and I was grateful that I could drop Cassie off in the morning on my way to school. If the sitter needed to take Cassie with her into town, she would dress her in Amish attire. Sometimes when I would pick Cassie up after school, she would still be in her little Amish outfit with her hair in short pigtails. I was thankful for the generosity of our Amish friends.

Obviously, my life was not like the average high schooler. It was difficult for me to connect with people at school and I wasn't hanging out with friends on a Friday night. Instead, Bruce and I were doing grown-up things like shopping for the week's groceries. With a baby and responsibilities, we had to grow up fast. The friends we knew in high school were still our friends, but we were just in different places in our lives. It was like we jumped ten years ahead, and so we started to surround ourselves with people ten years older than us who also had children.

During this time, we would see my family on occasion but spent more time with Bruce's family. We would attend church together on Sunday and often go over to their house for family meals. It was difficult for us to juggle Bruce's long hours of work, parenting a new baby, navigating married life, and my education. However, I was determined to finish school, and Bruce's family helped to motivate me. I remember Bruce's dad would often start a conversation with me and casually ask me about my grades on my report card. He probably didn't realize it, but that small talk motivated me to do better in school. My parents never asked about my grades. Bruce's family put a value on education that I didn't grow up with, and I was determined to make them proud.

In my senior year, I attended classes for the first part of the year and then was able to complete my schooling at home for the last several months. I did my school work and mailed in my assignments, which allowed me to be a stay-at-home mom. Bruce and I felt it was important that I stay home with Cassie instead of sending her off to a babysitter every day. I was grateful that I could complete my senior year at home and spend more time with our active toddler.

On June 10, 1995, I walked across the stage and received my high school diploma. It might sound like a cliché, but I beat the odds. It was no small feat to finish my high school education through my pregnancy and as a teenage mother. I am a living example that an unplanned pregnancy does not negatively define a person's future.

> **I AM A LIVING EXAMPLE THAT AN UNPLANNED PREGNANCY DOES NOT NEGATIVELY DEFINE A PERSON'S FUTURE.**

My whole school experience, since kindergarten, had been a constant struggle. I think back to all the days of school I had missed because of my family's continual uprooting. Though education was not a priority for my parents, God put people in my life who poured into me and showed me my worth. They motivated me to be better, and I knew education was important. If my life was to have a positive impact and if I wanted better for my kids, I knew that started with me. On my graduation day, Bruce held Cassie in his lap, and they watched me receive my diploma. I would be the only person in my family to graduate high school.

Bruce's family held a big graduation party at their house for Bruce's brother and me, as we both graduated on the same day. My family also threw me a small party, and my grandmother came from out of town. But we had even more to celebrate than my high school graduation. Just days before I graduated, we found out I was pregnant. We decided to keep it a secret from friends and family for a time.

Several weeks later, we told Cassie that she would be a big sister. She was only two years old, so we didn't know how much she understood. One day we went out to dinner with Bruce's family, and Cassie started to walk around the table and whisper in everyone's ear. As she whispered her secret, we watched as each person listened and then immediately smiled in our direction. Cassie decided to make our baby announcement for us that day. We couldn't have asked for a better way to announce that baby number two was on the way!

CHAPTER FIVE

This Is Us

He has made everything beautiful in its time.
He has also set eternity in the human heart;
yet no one can fathom what God has
done from beginning to end.
—ECCLESIASTES 3:11

We were eager to add to our little family. I was determined to be a good mom and wife. With Bruce working for his dad's construction business, I was able to be a stay-at-home mother to Cassie. My mom was proud of the fact that I was able to stay at home, as she was never able to for me and my sister. I felt like we were finally figuring things out, and with our new baby on the way, Bruce and I were excited about life.

However, there were signs in our marriage that things were not going so well. My insecurities seemed to build up walls between us and affected how we communicated. I struggled with my body image, feelings of doubt over being a good mother, and the unfounded fear that Bruce would leave me. Growing up in a home with constant fighting led to an irrational fear of abandonment. Even after two years of marriage, I struggled with letting Bruce in emotionally. If something made me upset, I would argue with him and then push him further away. I was caught in this trap of not knowing how to communicate in our marriage while at the same time wanting to be a good wife.

Despite our marriage struggles, our lives fell into a routine, and we were thrilled to move out of the apartment into our very first house. It was small and needed repairs, and the owners allowed Bruce to make all the renovations in exchange for rent. We loved our little home. It was located in the woods and had a nearby pond where we taught Cassie how to fish. We spent lots of time playing outside, and we were even able to have outdoor kittens for Cassie.

It was such a blessing that we could save money while living there rent-free. Bruce would come home from work and then put many hours into fixing up our little place. He worked hard for his family, and although at times I felt he spent too much time away, I was grateful for the sacrifices he made so that I could stay at home. Bruce was very good with our small budget, and I learned how to stretch what little money we had. Looking back, I see how God provided for us all along the way. There were difficult days with a limited budget, but we had all we needed.

CARTER

While I was pregnant, Bruce and I volunteered as youth leaders at our church, alongside the couple who mentored us in high school. On Sunday evenings, we would drop Cassie off with Bruce's family and lead the youth service. One night in

November, we were finishing up with the youth group when I started feeling some discomfort. We picked up Cassie and went home for the evening.

At midnight, I awoke to the mattress completely soaked beneath me. I woke Bruce up, and he immediately asked if I had wet myself. When I assured him that I did not have an accident, he began to look for a leak in our waterbed. It was an older model that someone had given to us, so that was a possibility. Reality finally set in that my water had broken and the baby was on the way! We packed Cassie into the car, dropped her off with Bruce's parents, and headed to the hospital.

I was ready to have this baby and welcome our new son or daughter, though we didn't know which it would be. We wanted to be surprised. I had a feeling we were going to have a boy, so we had picked out the name Carter since we were huge fans of the TV show *ER*, with the character named Dr. Carter. On the way to the hospital we panicked a little, thinking maybe we should have a girl's name picked out, too, just in case. There was no need. In the early morning hours of November 6, 1995, Carter Allen Dyksen arrived. We had a boy!

When Bruce got his first glimpse of Carter, however, he was alarmed. The umbilical cord had wrapped around our baby's neck and he was turning blue, but the doctor quickly cut the cord and unwrapped it from his little neck. What may be a weird twist in this birth story is that the doctor who delivered Carter is the same doctor who recommended my abortion to my parents when I was thirteen. He was my family doctor, as well as Bruce's family doctor. A different doctor delivered Cassie, but by the time Carter came along, we had changed to a familiar family physician.

Today, I question why it never occurred to me to make the connection that this doctor who delivered my son also suggested ending of the life of my first child. I keep coming back to the fact that although I went through the horrific experience of abortion, I didn't understand what abortion was in the broader sense. I was naïve about it all. But when there is no open discussion about the reality of abortion, there is no education that broadens your viewpoint.

> I DO KNOW I LIVED WITH FAR GREATER PAIN AND SUFFERING BECAUSE OF MY ABORTION. IS THAT HEALTHCARE?

After my abortion, no conversation, no counseling, and no emotional or spiritual healing of any kind had been offered to me. I lived in ignorance for so many years. Abortion wasn't discussed in my family, in my church, or even among my friends. I wasn't exposed to the pro-life viewpoint until much later, and no one in our circle talked about being "pro-life." Most people shied away from the conversation altogether.

Now I question how the same doctor could cut that umbilical cord to save Carter's life and yet not have an ethical problem with suggesting an abortion to end another life. These are discussions and questions we need to have in our society: in our churches, in our medical communities, and within our families. What if that doctor had instead suggested adoption services or referred my parents to the local pregnancy center? I don't like to live in the "what if" realm, but I do know I lived with far greater pain and suffering because of my abortion. Is that healthcare?

Despite the initial scare with the umbilical cord, we were thrilled that Carter was a healthy baby boy. My parents arrived to see their new grandson and spoiled Cassie so she wouldn't feel left out. Cassie loved her little brother, and they seemed to have a special bond from day one. Bruce's parents visited us when we arrived home. Carter was well loved by so many, and I loved being a mom to both a newborn and an active preschooler.

We lived as a family of four in our little home in the woods until Carter was about a year and a half old. Then we received an offer to live in a bigger house in town, again with a rent-free option. It was perfect timing since we were outgrowing our first home with two kids. Bruce made the needed renovations after work and on weekends, and we continued to add to our savings.

As the kids grew older, we began to think of the school system we wanted Cassie and Carter to attend. Bruce was driving about forty-five minutes back and forth to work, and he found a house for sale along his route. The community was located in the country, but the houses were close together. It was just the kind of neighborhood we were looking for and with the right schools. When I was twenty-three, we were able to buy our first home. Once again, God's provision for us was evident.

I am not sure how we were able to afford to be homeowners at such a young age other than the hand of God.

Bruce was making only eight dollars an hour, yet somehow that paid our mortgage and fed our family of four. Two healthy children and now a house of our very own. We counted our blessings.

HEALTH ISSUES

There was much to be thankful for, but I felt like our family wasn't quite complete. Bruce and I decided to try for another baby. At twenty-four years old, I was ecstatic to find out I was pregnant again. But my excitement was quickly over-shadowed one morning when I realized something was not right with the pregnancy. I called Bruce at work and asked him to take me to the doctor's office. He said he was over-whelmed with work projects and suggested I call a friend. I wanted him there with me, but I called my friend anyway. She sat in the waiting area while I had an ultrasound. The doctor couldn't locate the baby's heartbeat. I laid there after the procedure and began to sob.

I tried to put on a brave face for my friend as we drove home, pretending I was okay with the news, but I was devas-tated. The doctor sent me home to wait for the baby to mis-carry naturally, but when that didn't happen, I was sent to the hospital for a D&C (dilation and curettage) procedure. Bruce was able to come with me, and I was so thankful he was there.

Sadness overwhelmed me. My heart was broken in a mil-lion pieces. I remember driving home from the hospital and seeing a sign in someone's yard that read "Congrats, it's a boy!" Tears streamed down my face. Bruce looked over at me and asked what was wrong. *What was wrong?* I thought with frustration. I remember how upset I was at his reaction. *Was he not sad over the loss of our baby?* I felt alone with my grief and began pushing Bruce even further away. I struggled with depression after the loss, and Bruce went back to his job, working many long hours. I disconnected from him because I felt I couldn't go to him with my grief. He didn't seem to understand how the miscarriage affected me. It was hurtful, and I began to view Bruce as a villain who cared more about his work than about me. The walls between us seemed to build higher and higher in our marriage.

Around this time I began to realize that alcohol could easily numb my physical and emotional pain. I remember after my miscarriage having a drink and thinking, *I don't feel bad anymore.* It wasn't something that I turned to often at this time of my life, but it was a confirmation to me that if I needed to feel numb, alcohol would easily provide the desired effect.

In the fall of 2002, a single mom in our church was struggling with parenting her three boys. We knew the family and wanted to help them out. Our neighbor cared for the youngest child, and we agreed to take in the older boys. It was a private fostering agreement, and I was happy to open my home to more children. Despite my miscarriage, I still had the desire to love more children, and this was an opportunity that God seemed to provide for us at the time.

Our kids loved their foster brothers. Carter was in first grade when we decided to open our home to the two boys. One of the boys was in kindergarten, and the other was in third grade, the same age as Cassie. When Carter found out the boys would be living with us, he graciously gave up his bedroom to the two brothers. My mother-in-law was so impressed with Carter's selflessness that she submitted a story about his act of kindness to a Kohl's department store contest. He was selected and given an award along with scholarship money. We were proud of Carter, and we all enjoyed providing a home to help a family in need.

During this same time, I began struggling with health issues. My reproductive health seemed to be failing, and I was continually battling pain every month. I would go to different doctors, but they would have no real answers for me. One night as we were watching a speech by President George Bush on television, I felt something pop inside of me and suddenly had excruciating pain. Bruce called the OB-GYN doctor's office, and they told me to go directly to the emergency room, so he then called his mom to come watch the kids. By then I had started hemorrhaging and was losing lots of blood. When we arrived at the emergency room, they rushed me to an exam room and performed an ultrasound. My pelvis was full of blood. They said I needed surgery immediately or I might die. The doctor warned me of the possible outcomes of the operation, including having an ovary removed or a complete hysterectomy. They had no idea what they would find but would do whatever was needed to save my life.

I woke up to the news that my left ovary had ruptured and had to be removed. After another night in the hospital I was released, very sore and weak but grateful that the surgery was not as drastic as expected. I settled in at home, ready to rest and recuperate. The next morning, however, Bruce asked if it would be all right if he went back to work. I didn't see why not as I thought I could handle things. The kids went to school two hours apart, so I planned to take my time getting them all ready for school and then relaxing the rest of the day. But while I was helping the kids, I suddenly passed out on the floor.

Alarmed, the kids ran to the neighbor's house to get help, and I awoke to find my neighbor praying over me. She had called Bruce, and he came home and rushed me back to the hospital. I had lost so much blood from the ruptured ovary that I needed a blood transfusion. This time, I spent a couple more nights in the hospital recuperating and building up my strength.

If only that were the end of my health problems. Unfortunately, there was no relief from the ongoing reproductive pain I experienced. Even though I wanted another baby, it just didn't seem possible. The foster boys went back to live with their mother, leaving me longing to add to our family. Soon we were approached about a potential adoption opportunity, and my heart braced for the hope of having another baby.

My sister-in-law had a college friend who had been raped and was pregnant and chose life for her child. The mother wanted a family to adopt her baby. Our home was open and ready for us to adopt. We wanted to be there for someone in their time of need and I longed for another baby. I was so excited about this opportunity. I took Cassie to a store to look for nursery items. We purchased an outfit for the baby, picked out bedding, and made preparations. Our family was thrilled about welcoming a little one into our home.

However, it wasn't long before we received a call that the mother had a miscarriage. My heart was broken, again. It seemed it wasn't meant to be that we would have another child.

With two children to care for, I tried to push through the sadness filling my days, but the emotional and physical pain were building up. Maybe they were connected. I still held on to emotional scars. I had never received counseling for my past sexual abuse or healing from the abortion. The family turmoil I grew up in had created deep roots that were manifesting in my marriage. It was as if layer upon layer was being added, and I was carrying the heavy burden of all the layers of trauma, pain, and dysfunction. Was all of this now affecting my physical health? All I knew for sure was that it was mentally exhausting to experience daily physical pain without any answers.

The doctors diagnosed my symptoms as endometriosis. It almost seemed as if they didn't know what I had, so they labeled it a common medical condition. Regardless, I had reached my limit with the continual pain. When a doctor eventually suggested a hysterectomy, Bruce and I felt that if it would finally end all my suffering, it would be worth it. So at age twenty-nine, I had a complete hysterectomy, ushering in early menopause with its hot flashes and accompanying symptoms. I had always wanted more children, but that door was now officially closed.

As I write about this time in my life, the hurt still feels fresh. I was so young to have a hysterectomy. My womb was closed while many women my age were just beginning to have babies. It didn't seem fair. But now I see God's plan even in the painful and seemingly unjust circumstances. We were blessed with two beautiful, healthy children.

I think about young teenagers who face unplanned pregnancies, as I did. The first question is often, "What about my future?" Their hopes and aspirations tend to diminish with news of a pregnancy. Even their parents often view their future with a negative outcome. But we don't know the future;

God does. He knew my health issues. He knew when my womb would be closed. The Giver of life gives life for a reason with a purpose.

Cassie and Carter are living out their purpose today because of God's perfect plan.

Ecclesiastes 3:11 says, "He has made everything beautiful in its time. He has also set eternity in the human heart; yet no one can fathom what God has done from beginning to end."

Though our circumstances were unplanned from our perspective, they were always part of our loving Creator's perfect and eternal plan for us. While we might not have been able to fathom what God could do, we are continually learning to trust in that perfect, purposeful plan.

> I HAD NEVER RECEIVED COUNSELING FOR MY PAST SEXUAL ABUSE OR HEALING FROM THE ABORTION.

LAYER UPON LAYER

Though I was thankful for our two children, I struggled with deepening depression after my hysterectomy. I had no desire to go on social outings, to church, or even to Bruce's parents' house for dinner. It was easier to shut everyone out than to put on a happy face and make-believe I was okay. The person I shut out the most was Bruce. It was all based on my insecurities and fears. I didn't know my worth, and I thought I could be replaced at any moment. I was plagued by the thought, *Bruce deserves better than me.* I couldn't accept that he truly loved me, and in turn, I responded in very hurtful ways. It was so much easier to keep enforcing that wall around my heart than to be completely open and vulnerable in our marriage.

> WHEN WE VIEW ABORTION WITH A BROAD SCOPE, WE SEE THE DEVASTATING EFFECTS AND HOW MANY PEOPLE IT HURTS.

Around the same time as my health issues, my parents' marriage was falling apart. They had moved to Illinois for a time, but my mother became an emotional wreck and threatened to end her life with a gun that was in their house. My father ended up moving back to Indiana while she remained in Illinois. My mother eventually moved back in with him, and they lived together for a short time. Then one day he left a note on the table saying he was sorry and disappeared. Later we found out he had moved to Texas with another woman.

My mother and sister had a huge falling out, and my whole family just fell apart. It was as if the weight of constant dysfunction finally broke. We moved my mother closer to us to be available to help as she continued to battle her physical and emotional health issues.

As I think back to my mother's ongoing mental struggles and all my health problems, I still question where my abortion factors into all of this. I don't have a medical degree and haven't researched this topic in-depth, but I have heard story after story of other women who have had similar health issues to mine. They all had abortions, and they all suffered from many reproductive complications—some with early hysterectomies. Physical and mental health complications are common consequences of abortion, and many women can testify to the truth of that statement. But I also wonder about what my mother went through. How did it affect her to hear her young daughter scream in the abortion clinic? Or to learn about my sexual abuse? When we view abortion with a broad scope, we see the devastating effects and how many people it hurts.

I felt like I was navigating through rough waters with all these issues. Layer upon layer continued to build up in my life. I kept searching for answers. There was something missing but I didn't know what. Despite my ongoing depression and health issues, I went to church and volunteered; I knew God and His Word, and I prayed, yet something was missing. I understood salvation, but my heart still didn't make the connection of just how much God loved me. I realize now that I was searching for freedom. But unfortunately, there were too many layers of hurt and pain for me to understand how to break through the walls that I had allowed to encompass me.

Despite everything, God was graciously providing for our family. I did see the blessings even amid the trials. I knew how fortunate I was to be able to stay home with our kids, and I enjoyed being a mom and wife despite all my insecurities. Carter and Cassie were active middle schoolers, and their activities kept our family busy. Life seemed to go on as usual until a phone call completely blindsided me.

In the summer of 2010, Bruce and I were sitting at our kitchen table when he shared with me some disturbing news from a phone conversation he had. He mentioned a rumor that he had heard about one of our friends, who was also our neighbor. The words he spoke left me speechless. I heard him say that Henry (not his real name) had been accused of sexually abusing someone. I could not believe it. He was our friend and a person we trusted. Those words cut my soul deeply and sent me into a tailspin.

CHAPTER SIX

Unhealed

No, in all these things we are more than conquerors through him who loved us.
—ROMANS 8:37

A s soon as I heard the words "sexual abuse," I felt a wave of anger welling up deep inside of me. Henry was a respected member of our community. He was the neighbor everyone could count on to help out. An avid outdoorsman, Henry enjoyed bowhunting, archery, and target shooting with rifles. It was not uncommon for him to teach kids how to do this type of sport. Just thinking about that brought my memory back to my uncle giving me "driving lessons." Raw emotions were gripping me.

THE STORM

Shortly after hearing the rumors about our neighbor, a severe thunderstorm hit our area. Several trees were damaged on our street, and we lost power. Henry dropped by to check up on us after the storm, and I pretended like everything was fine. It was so difficult to go through the motions of trying to be a friendly neighbor. All I wanted to know was, did he do what was alleged?

It seemed odd that a bad storm hit our area at the same time we found out about Henry's abuse. Our small community was shocked and stunned by the news. It was as if two storms simultaneously hit our neighborhood. I felt like a ton of bricks hit me. Hearing that my neighbor had possibly sexually abused anyone was enough to take me over the edge. I couldn't even explain my reaction at the time, but it triggered fear, shame, guilt, and anger. I knew there was a deeper reason behind my rage, but I wasn't ready to deal with those feelings.

Around this same time, Bruce was in charge of leading a volunteer firefighter training where Henry was also a volunteer. Bruce had asked me to help serve lunch at the training event. I didn't want to help and asked Bruce to cancel the training exercise. I was not doing well emotionally, and I knew I could not face Henry at the fire station. But when Bruce is committed to something, the decision is usually final, and it is typically difficult for him to change gears. I was mad at Bruce because I felt he was not listening to me. It seemed as if he was choosing the fire department over his wife and ignoring how much I was struggling.

Reluctantly, I went to the training and helped serve lunch. They had various stations set up so the firemen could practice their skills. Of course, Henry was there, and the first thing I noticed was he was hanging around a kid at the training exercises. I wanted to march right over there, punch him in the face, and snatch that child away from him. It turned out that I didn't have to. Henry had received a call and left the training in a hurry. The police were waiting for him at his house. There were about ten police cars parked in his driveway and in front of his house. Our whole community was buzzing over the day's events—first because of all the fire trucks on their training exercises, and then because of all the police cars gathered on our street.

Our whole neighborhood was shocked by Henry's arrest. He had duped everyone, including me. His arrest began to divide the neighborhood because it was a hard pill to swallow that a "pillar in the community" could break our trust like that.

Henry was released on bail and was allowed back in his house in our neighborhood. I had so much hatred in my heart for this man. I was really angry. How could I have missed it? If I had known he was a sexual predator, I would have never become friends with the man. I was upset with myself for never noticing the signs.

During this time, I began working as a paraprofessional for a Special Education class in a local school. These were kids I had grown to love through working at the school, and one of them had been abused by Henry. My heart ached for that young man! I will forever have a heart for the kids and adults who live a down-and-out kind of life. I was that type of kid. Henry had hurt this student, and the boy was struggling. The mama bear in me was filled with rage. As a victim of sexual abuse myself, I never wanted to see another person have to go through what I did. I had so much shame and guilt; I feel like I should have known about Henry.

The court proceedings in Henry's case were a long, drawn-out process for several reasons, but mostly because of ongoing court congestion. We quickly learned that the people sitting in jail are entitled to a speedy trial, so they go first. Since Henry was out on bond, the case would have to wait. It would be over a year before we found out any conclusion. The whole process made Bruce and me often ask the question, *What about the right to a fair and speedy trial for the victims, not just the accused?*

TRAPPED

In the meantime, I wanted to move and get our family out of that neighborhood. Just the mention of the term "sex abuser" made me feel unsafe. I could not live in a community with that monster. Bruce did not agree with me, and he was having a difficult time understanding just how much this was affecting me. I started to build up resentment toward Bruce. He seemed to be able to move on with life, and it felt like he didn't care how much my heart hurt. He was serving at church and as a volunteer fireman and had an active role in our community. He refused to move. I couldn't understand how he could be comfortable with this situation. What was not being communicated, however, was that Bruce knew we could not afford to move. I was not aware of our financial situation, and this lack of communication created a conflict cycle in our marriage. We just kept going round and round. We both wanted off this crazy ride, but we didn't have the understanding or tools to accomplish it. We knew we needed help, but we didn't even know what kind of help we needed.

I felt trapped living in a neighborhood with a sexual predator just a few houses down the road. I was paranoid about allowing my children, who were teenagers at the time, to go outside for even a quick jog in the neighborhood. I became obsessed with making sure Henry never hurt another person again. I hated the man. I viewed him as a piece of trash. I'm embarrassed to say this now, but I would drive by his house and throw garbage in his yard; I wanted him to know he was trash for what he did. People who abuse kids should go to jail. He was not fit for society. My heart became so dark.

I began to direct much of my anger toward Bruce. Our marriage was becoming a wreck. I couldn't control my feelings of rage and hurt, so I shifted the blame to others around me, especially to Bruce. He had no idea why I was responding the way I was to the situation with our neighbor. Bruce was unaware of my deep, unhealed trauma. My wounds were so deep from my sexual abuse that once they started to open, it was like an erupting volcano, and the molten lava was falling on everyone around me. It was affecting not only my marriage but how I parented my kids. I felt like a terrible mom. I was not parenting well, and my kids deserved better. I was hurting so deeply and felt so broken, but I didn't know how to change it.

I soon realized I had to stop working due to all the stress in my life. My heart was too broken and shattered to work at the school. I would look at all the students and wonder if they were being abused. It was driving me insane, and I couldn't move past it. I was exhausted by my anger. There were many days that I lay in bed and refused to get up. I remember one day, Bruce invited one of my dear friends to come over to pray with me. She sat next to me and tried so hard to encourage me to press into the Lord. But I was stuck, and I didn't know how to reach out to God. It was like I was in a deep, dark hole that I couldn't get out of. I was depressed, bitter, and so very angry. I quickly turned to the one thing that I knew could temporarily numb my pain—alcohol.

At first, I started going to bars with friends, but that turned into drinking every day at home. One day, Bruce mentioned something about my excessive drinking, and I became so angry. "How dare you?" I questioned him sharply. He had every right to question my behavior and bad choices, but in my rage, I felt I had every right to numb my pain.

I began to view Bruce as an unsafe person for our family for not protecting us. I couldn't get past the fact that he would not move our family out of the neighborhood and away from danger. We fought all the time, and I pushed him further and further away. I wouldn't allow myself to be close to him. As my anger increased toward Bruce, my boundaries to protect my marriage decreased. I started to connect with someone I knew online. At first, he was just someone with whom I could vent all my frustrations. I wanted someone to listen to me, and he was easy to talk to. But I began to compare my relationship with him to my marriage with Bruce. Looking back, I should have never started that online conversation. As innocent as it seemed, it was a boundary I crossed. It was unhealthy, and it divided my marriage even more.

While I was spiraling out of control, Bruce was trying to cope the best he could with his pain. "I put my head down and pushed through," Bruce recalls. "I knew I needed to remain calm and provide a healthy home." Bruce was intentionally calm because he was very aware of his temper. As a boy, his mother was concerned about his anger. "I remember my mom saying to me that if I don't control myself, I might kill someone. Her words stuck with me. I am grateful for her wisdom and counsel that helped me through painful times where I might have let my temper get the best of me."

Bruce too was struggling, just not in the same way as me. I was full of rage and was drinking and acting out. He tried to keep it all together for our family's sake, trying to persevere the best he could. Bruce remarked, "I remember having a list of praise songs that I would listen to on a job site while I was alone to help me through the day. Sometimes the words of the songs would bring me to tears. I remember asking God, *Why me?* I cried out to God to save my family from this mess. I tried so hard to be a good father, husband, and provider, and it always felt like I could never get to the finish line."

The tensions in our marriage kept building. We fought often about money, mainly about why we couldn't move. At one point we did sign a purchase agreement to buy another house. Bruce recalls the mistake in that decision: "I turned over every stone to try to get help with a down payment. I asked friends, my grandmother, and even begged my banker. No one would help. I eventually had to call my realtor and back out of the agreement. I knew we were too financially strapped to move. The realtor was upset and threatened to sue me for breaking the contract. The owner kept our five hundred dollar deposit, and I wrote him an apology letter."

JUSTICE

While I was dealing with depression, I was still focused on the ongoing criminal proceedings. Time dragged on, and we waited another nine months for the case to conclude. When I finally heard the news that Henry—despite being found guilty—would serve no jail time, I was dumbfounded. The sentence infuriated me. Bruce and I began to have a discussion in the car over the outcome. I looked at Bruce, and he didn't seem angry at all. The conversation turned into a huge fight. My heart was pounding out of my chest with rage, but Bruce seemed settled with the results. "Why aren't you upset about this?" I challenged him. Once again, he looked at everything with logic and reason. I, on the other hand, wondered how he could remain calm about the lack of justice that was just handed down.

For me, that was a point of no return with Bruce. I already felt I couldn't trust him. I wanted a reaction from him that conveyed he was just as angry as I was. In retrospect, I can see how God was using Bruce, with his calm demeanor, but I didn't see it that way at the time. All I saw was a man who refused to show any kind of reaction. I then proceeded to kick Bruce out of the car. That is the day I became a runner. I ran straight to friends who would listen to my frustrations and who saw nothing wrong with me drinking my sorrows away.

I desperately wanted justice served. I didn't know why but it was everything to me. Maybe it was a deep-seated feeling that justice had never been served in my own life. All I could think about was the abuse. I hated that this event consumed me, but I didn't know how to get out of it. Day after

> **I DIDN'T REACH FOR HIM AT THE TIME, BUT GOD WAS ABOUT TO SHOW ME REAL VICTORY AND JUSTICE.**

day, I was living in hell, and I didn't know how to fix me. I was drowning in fear, shame, and doubt and spewing hatred at my husband—a safe person in my life. But Bruce didn't feel safe to me; nothing felt safe or controlled in my life.

Looking back on this time in my life, it reminded me how hearing those two words about Henry—"sexual abuse"—triggered such brokenness in me. That event caused my life to spiral out of control because I was unhealed. Hearing those words and knowing how others around me were hurting pulled me full force into victim mode. I didn't understand that God created me to be a victor and to live in freedom, as Romans 8:37 says: "No, in all these things we are more than conquerors through him who loved us."

One of my favorite worship songs mentions singing in the midst of a storm and finding hope rise from the ashes. I didn't know how to sing in the middle of the storm that struck my community. All I knew were ashes because I didn't understand the healing work of Jesus Christ. But while everything was falling apart in my life, God was there. I didn't reach for him at the time, but God was about to show me real victory and justice.

CHAPTER SEVEN

Lavished Love

But by the grace of God I am what I am,
and his grace to me was not without effect.
—1 Corinthians 15:10

Our home was now a place of continual stress and turmoil for me. Even with the court proceedings winding down, I was still stuck. I struggled daily with depression and anger. My marriage was falling apart, and I continued to push Bruce further and further away. I began spending less time at home and more time finding anyone willing to party with me to numb all my emotional pain with alcohol.

Eventually, Bruce decided we could financially move to a new house. It's what I had wanted all along—to move from the neighborhood where all the trauma took place. I thought a new home would mean a fresh start for all of us. But what I realized was a new house didn't solve anything for me. It was a new location, but the same me wallowing in my misery and bitterness and holding on to feelings of rage that I just couldn't shake.

MOVING OUT

On the day I kicked Bruce out of the car, something had hardened inside of me. I'd had enough. I had been looking for someone as the culprit of my anger and decided Bruce was it. If the move to a new house didn't help, then nothing would, so I eventually decided that leaving our new home was my answer and moved out.

During this time, I was working as a therapy assistant in a nursing home. I would finish work for the day and find other employees—or anyone—willing to have a drink with me. With those I drank with, I found a sympathetic audience. I felt supported by these people, even though nothing positive was changing in my life. I would drink, crash for the night at a friend's house, and start all over again the next day. Eventually, a friend of mine who was going through a divorce offered me her spare bedroom. I decided to move in with her.

My friends and family were naturally worried about me. I would get text messages throughout the day from my kids, my sister-in-law, Bruce's cousin Heather, who I was close with, and others who saw a negative change in me and were concerned about my behavior. Although Cassie pushed me away because of my actions, Carter tried to stay connected with me but I kept him at a distance while I was trapped in my mess. We were all hurting and it was a painful time.

Bruce was always reaching out and urging me to come back home. He wanted us to try to work on our marriage. One day he came over to my friend's house after a snow storm, and I watched from the window as he cleaned the snow off my car and shoveled the driveway. He knew I hated the cold weather and was making an effort to show me kindness. I showed him no compassion in return. I wanted him to leave me alone. He would try everything to convince me to move back home, but I didn't want to. My trust was broken, and I felt unsafe around him. What I didn't realize was that Bruce was struggling too and was working hard to keep his family together.

"It was all so frustrating for me," Bruce recalls. "I moved our family to a new neighborhood for Serena. I did not love our new home but settled into it because she said the move would fix everything. When she left, I remember throwing and breaking things out in our backyard. I yelled, argued, and cried out to God. All I wanted was for God to restore our marriage."

At this point, it felt too late for us. I was resentful watching Bruce fight for our marriage. I kept thinking, *Why did it take me leaving for him to be strong and fight for our family?* I realize now what a lie that was straight from the enemy. Bruce was leading our family well but I took over the leadership in our home and made a mess of things. I was trying to control things because my life was out of control. The devil was blinding me and pitting us against each other, and I was falling right into his trap.

One day I called Bruce at home and we ended up arguing over the phone. Our discussion got heated, and I started cursing at him. He then directed the kids into our conversation, and I realized our heated exchange was being heard over the speakerphone. He intended to have an intervention with the kids reaching out to me, but it backfired. Cassie and Carter heard every angry word spoken, and it crushed me. I already felt like a terrible mother, and that made me feel worse. I wanted to see and spend time with Cassie and Carter, but I felt like I didn't deserve to be their mother. I was embarrassed by my behavior and hated the situation I was in. That plunged me further into my pit, and by this time, I was not only drinking daily but misusing prescription drugs and smoking synthetic marijuana.

It was difficult for me to comprehend how I could get to such a low point in my life. As a kid, I learned that when trouble comes, we run. My parents would rather move to a new house, drink, smoke, turn to food, or blame others than deal with their problems. I said I wanted better for my own family; things would be different for me. But those coping habits eventually followed me into adulthood. The very thing I was determined not to do, I ended up doing: I was running from my problems.

While I was trapped in my cycle of misery, Bruce tried to keep things stable at home with the kids. He also reached out to two pastors at church who prayed with him and counseled him, yet he often felt alone. "It especially hit me hard when I had to sit by myself at church on Sunday mornings," Bruce remembers. "There were several times that I would just sit there and begin to cry."

But God did encourage Bruce during our difficult time of separation. Bruce received a call from a local pastor seeking a contractor for some work to be done on his church. Bruce met the pastor for an estimate and in the process shared our family story with him. "I just started spilling my heart out to the pastor for some reason," Bruce shared. "I never did end up doing the contract work for the church, but the pastor would often call or text to check up on me and tell me he was praying for me. It meant so much to know that someone who barely knew me was praying for my family

and me. It felt like a divine appointment. God placed someone in my life at a very dark time so I would know I was not
alone in this struggle."

As for me, I felt I was at a point of no return with my
family. I was out partying every single weekend, drinking
every single day, and would use drugs if I could get my hands
on them. I was out of control and wanted to feel nothing at
all. One particular evening, I had planned a typical night out
with friends. We met at a local restaurant, and before going
in, one friend and I smoked some weed in the parking lot
and got high. We then joined the rest of our group inside,
and for the next three hours, we had one drink after another.
As the night went on, I realized I had crossed a line; there
was no way I could drive home, and I didn't want to risk getting pulled over by the police.

Sitting in the restaurant, I texted some friends asking
them to pick me up. A couple of them texted me back and
said I needed to get my act together. I questioned, *Who do
they think they are, telling me what to do?* I knew my friends
were right, but their words stung, and shame smacked me
right in the face. I had done this before, and I just expected
people to come to my rescue. I was selfish, and my self-
centered behavior was catching up with me. My friends were
tired of my two a.m. rescue calls. Through text messages they
were speaking truth, which I desperately needed to hear, but
it infuriated me. I reacted by drinking some more.

RADICAL ENCOUNTER

I eventually staggered out to my car in the parking lot. I sat
inside and started texting more people out of desperation. I
would either get no response or a firm "no" in reply. I had

burned so many bridges with people: my kids, Bruce, family members, and even the same people who were once willing to drink and party with me. I sat there in the middle of the night in my red Honda CRV and broke down in tears. I was a drunken mess, and no one was willing to help me.

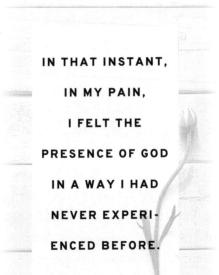

IN THAT INSTANT, IN MY PAIN, I FELT THE PRESENCE OF GOD IN A WAY I HAD NEVER EXPERIENCED BEFORE.

At that moment, my life had come full circle sitting in the same car I had kicked Bruce out of, but now I had nowhere to go. I was trapped with no one to rescue me, no safety net—nothing. It was just me broken and busted in my dark pit, and I didn't know how to get out of it. I hated who I had become. How did I even get to such a low spot? When you are at your breaking point, you don't take stock of every action, every pain, or every traumatic moment in your life. You just instinctively know that you need to break free. The burden I was carrying was so heavy, and I was so exhausted. I sat there feeling defeated and began to weep uncontrollably. With despair and emptiness, I cried out, "God, I have nothing left but you. Please, I need your help!"

In that instant, in my pain, I felt the presence of God in a way I had never experienced before. It was an indescribable feeling. The best way to describe it is that I felt utterly lavished by the love of God. He met me there in my car, and I wasn't alone. I was safe. My heavenly Father wrapped me in his arms with this feeling of comfort that I will never forget. His love lifted me out of my dark pit. I was no longer drowning. For so long, I felt dead inside. I would go through the motions of each day, but I felt such emptiness. But that simple prayer brought me life. There was this feeling of hope, and I knew—right then and there—that God had answered my prayer.

The next thing I felt was God directing me to go home. Not to my friend's house with a spare bedroom, but home to Bruce and my family. God's hand of protection was on me that night. I barely remember driving home, but I made it safely to the driveway of my house. I pressed the garage door opener and found Bruce standing in the doorway. When I got out of the car, he immediately embraced me. There were no words of confrontation, just his open arms extended toward me. Bruce hugged me and held me close to him. I cried with a sense of reassurance in his arms. That night, God met me with his indescribable love and mercy toward me. I finally found God's grace, but I also received my husband's grace.

CHAPTER EIGHT

Healing Begins

You, Lord, took up my case;
you redeemed my life.
—LAMENTATIONS 3:58

W hen I returned home, I decided to let go of my bitterness toward Bruce. I was tired of fighting all the
demons in my life. Jesus had met me, and I felt his love. All I
wanted was more of that love in my life. Bruce and I had a
lot of healing to work through, and we knew we couldn't do
it on our own. We would have to put our pride aside and ask
God for help and seek counseling.

I asked Bruce to give me some time and space. I was so
wounded that surrendering all of my pain was difficult. It
was a slow process and I needed time to work through my
emotions. He tried to be supportive, but he was also very
guarded with me. "This was the third time I had extended
grace to Serena," Bruce recalls. "I wasn't sure she would stay.
Actually, I doubted how all of it would turn out. There might

have been a small change in Serena, but I sensed we still needed to work through a lot of things."

THE WORD

My radical encounter with God was something I couldn't shake. I wanted more of him, and I knew I could find the answers in the Word of God. I didn't know exactly where the answers were in the Scriptures, so I searched the Internet for verses and their meaning. The more I read, the more God began to reveal himself to me, and I couldn't get enough of it. The Bible became my first step toward healing.

I journaled Scripture after Scripture and began saying the passages out loud. In those moments, God was teaching me to stand on his truth. I would walk around my house during the day, having battle cries against the enemy and reciting Bible verses. I am sure if anyone had seen me, they would have thought I was crazy. It was a wonderful time of just me and God. I was sitting at his feet, soaking in his Word, and learning who I was in him. God's Word was not only encouraging me but giving me hope.

Through Scripture, I was learning to fight my battles. My spiritual journey was coming full circle. When I was in fifth grade, Mr. Whistler told me about Jesus, took me to church, and gave me my first Bible. He planted a spiritual seed within me. When I was pregnant with Cassie, I started to attend church again. I thought I knew who Jesus was, but when I fell into my emotional pit of hell, I didn't know how to get out. I had some knowledge of Jesus Christ but didn't know how to seek him in my turmoil. He seemed so far away from me. Did God really love me? Did he see that my heart was broken in a million pieces?

As I searched the Scriptures, I realized that I had been running to everything but God. I wasn't reading his Word, I stopped attending church, and I wasn't praying. God was there all along. He never left me, but he was waiting for me to call out to him. God doesn't force us to have a relationship with him. He patiently waits on us, and when we call out to him, he answers. I was rescued from my pit by God's grace, and the more I dug into the Bible, the more he began to apply a healing balm in my life.

Bruce witnessed my daily digging into God's Word. "I would see her studying, which brought her internal healing," he recalled, "but it took a while for it to bear fruit. But once it did, it had a snowball effect in her life."

I smile now when I think about Mr. Whistler giving me that Bible when I was a young girl. He pointed me toward Jesus Christ. That Bible was one of the books I reached for as I searched for answers. Mr. Whistler had no idea of the tragic experiences I would face in my life: my rape, my abortion, my health problems, and my marriage struggles. But what he did know was that all I needed was in the pages of that Bible. My Savior's love was healing me with every Scripture verse.

BACK TO CHURCH

Reading the Bible was just the beginning of my healing. I also started Christian counseling and committed to attending church again with Bruce. But going back to church proved more difficult than I had expected. My first day back was on Easter Sunday. It took all the courage I could find to walk through the doors of my church building. The thoughts in my head had kept me away: *Everyone is going to look at you disapprovingly. You are still a mess, and people are going to reject you.* I wondered what people were saying behind my back. But I pushed through and decided Easter Sunday would be the day.

As soon as I entered the front doors of the church with Bruce, I had a full-on panic attack. All I wanted to do was bolt and run right out of there. I felt a weight on my chest, like heavy chains were strapped around me. I know now that I was under intense spiritual warfare. Satan was speaking lies in my thoughts, filling my head with all kinds of anxiety about the people in the church.

> **AS I WORSHIPED, THE HEAVY CHAINS FELL RIGHT OFF OF ME, AND I PUSHED THROUGH THE LIES OF THE ENEMY'S ATTACK.**

The best way to describe this anxiety was that I felt like my mask had been taken off and I worried, *How could I expose myself to all the Christians in that room?* What I knew about church was that we get all dressed up, put on makeup, do our hair, slap a smile on our face, and tell everyone we are doing just fine. We don't share our deep, dark secrets in the church because we are scared of what people might think of us. That was me. But I wasn't fine; I was still struggling, still healing, and my mask was coming off.

Bruce calmly encouraged me to walk into the seating area, and we finally sat down. I still wanted to run out the door, but I knew Bruce wouldn't let me. He suddenly got up from his seat and disappeared for several minutes. While I sat there clutching my chair with tension and fear, Bruce reached out to some of the pastors and leaders of the church. He shared with them that I was struggling, and they began covering me in prayer at that moment.

It was during that service that God beautifully met me once again. I don't remember the worship songs or the pastor's sermon, but I do recall lifting my hands to praise my Jesus in worship as I had never done before. I felt his presence all around me. As I worshiped, the heavy chains fell right off of me, and I pushed through the lies of the enemy's attack. My husband fought for me the best way he could—by bringing others into my battle through prayer. Those prayers were answered. In that moment of worship, I made a choice: I could keep running, pretending, and doing the same thing over and over again, or I could call out to God for help. I chose the latter, and I began to put in the work to heal and to find complete freedom.

Soon after I began attending church again, Bruce signed us up for a Dynamic Marriage course. Right away, I realized I did not want to be a part of the class. I was still struggling with what other people thought of me, and I went into that course with a big chip on my shoulder. Why would I want these people to know all of our mess? It was hard, but I stuck with it.

The marriage course was painful and yet healing at the same time. We both had to unpack a lot of hurt in our marriage. As we progressed through the class, we experienced some beautiful moments together learning how to communicate and relate to one another. Years later, I would talk to other couples who took that class with us. Many of their marriages were also a mess and were falling apart, but at the time, no one wanted to share what we were all experiencing. It was encouraging to know that we were not the only couple struggling in our marriage, but I wish I had known that back then.

Pretending and putting on a mask—inside and outside of the church—was exhausting. I had worn that mask for so long, and eventually I crashed and burned. But asking for prayer, going to counseling, and realizing that it was okay to not be okay were all part of being a follower of Jesus Christ. I needed a lot of help. There were layers upon layers still left to go and pain to work through. But I was ready. And with every step closer I got to God, there was less chaos in my life.

COUNSELING

Even though I had a radical encounter with God and was spiritually growing in Christ daily, I still needed proper spiritual guidance to deal with some deeper issues. Scheduling a counseling session was the easy part, but getting the courage to go to my appointment turned out to be quite a challenge.

It was so difficult to sit in the counselor's room and get into the nitty-gritty parts of my life. It was hard work to be transparent, to discuss things that I didn't want to talk about with anyone. I fought it every single time I had an appointment and was notorious for canceling at the last minute. On the morning of a meeting, I would begin to talk myself out of going. Then I would say to myself, *This is stupid, I have to go.* I would arrive for my session but sit in my car in the parking lot, listing reasons in my head why I should not go in. It took courage to make myself walk into my counselor's office. I'd sit down, hug some pillows, and pack as much security around me as I could.

Some of the sessions included Bruce to help strengthen our marriage. During those sessions, I began to target Bruce, blaming him for everything falling apart in my life. For a while we would go together, but it didn't take long before the counselor transitioned to just wanting to meet with me alone. This change made me angry. I thought, *Oh, I see. I am the problem!* But deep down, I knew it was ultimately about me. I was a mess and needed help first, to be able to move forward in our marriage.

The most challenging part of my sessions was when the counselor brought Jesus into our conversation. It sounds crazy. Yes, I had a radical encounter with God, and I was feeling the saving power of Jesus Christ in my life, but I didn't want to talk about him. I would shut down at the mention of his name. My counselor would say, "Okay, we don't have to go there." And ten minutes later, in the most gentle way, he would bring Jesus right back into the conversation.

Here's the truth about my conflict with the name of Jesus. Even though God had lavished his love on me, it was hard to really understand and accept that love. Being transparent was difficult because of a fear that if I were truly honest about all of my deep, dark secrets, God would not love me. How could he possibly love someone as broken as me? I had been abandoned as a young girl, mistreated, and sexually abused. I craved a father's love. My earthly father didn't have that kind of love for me, so how could Jesus? That was the lie Satan used in my life—over and over again—to keep me from being free. But the truth of the matter was, God already knew my secrets and loved me anyway. He saw everything I had gone through and had done, and he wept. God never wanted to see me—his child—go through the things I did. He saw that I was hurting, and he was holding out his hand the whole time.

It was easy to turn my attention to God's Word and to reach out to him *on my terms.* But allowing God to fill me with his unconditional love, completely letting my guard down, was so difficult for me. Embracing the name of Jesus in my counseling sessions was doing the hard work of letting go of fear, shame, lies, pride, and feelings of unworthiness, and grabbing on to that outstretched hand of God.

The next stage in my counseling was therapy for deep trauma victims called Eye Movement Desensitization and Reprocessing (EMDR). This counseling involved deep inner healing therapy and prayer. It was at this stage that I faced the traumatic events of my childhood. I had never received help in the form of counseling on how to process the traumatic sexual abuse in my life. Growing up with a history of sexual abuse in my family, I learned all about the shame and guilt wrapped up in that history. I was taught that we don't talk about painful experiences. Unpacking those memories as an adult was unloading layer upon layer of deep-seated emotional pain, built up over so many years. Those layers of trauma were being peeled back, and it was painful.

When you are sexually abused, you don't want to talk about your past. You just don't! It is so incredibly difficult, and unless you experience it, you can't understand the shame and hindrance in speaking out. I didn't realize I could be free from my past. I had to learn to trust that God was who he said he was in my life. I didn't need to put on a mask and pretend everything was okay. Now I was learning to stand on

God's truth and declare it over my life. I am so thankful for EMDR counseling. It was the profound healing I needed to find real change and direction.

However, there was one area of my life that I was not willing to share in these counseling sessions. I never brought up my abortion. As I began digging deeper into my sexual abuse, the counselor asked me if there was any other trauma I needed to share with him. I wanted to tell him, but I could not bring myself to say it out loud. I don't recall talking about my abortion since telling Bruce in the parking lot of Planned Parenthood at fifteen years old. I don't know why I was not willing to dig deeper at that time, except for the fact that it was such a painful past event, and I just wasn't ready.

"AHA" MOMENTS

There were days I still struggled, but if I had thoughts of Satan's lies in my head, I knew the steps to take. I prayed and searched the Word of God, declaring Scripture over my life to remind the enemy about the truths of God that protected me. As I began to heal, God would reveal himself in surprising ways, and I would have these Holy Spirit–directed aha moments that brought healing and forgiveness into my life. The first aha moment came when I realized I had elevated Bruce to an unrealistic position in our marriage.

When I was fifteen years old in the parking lot of Planned Parenthood, as Bruce supported my decision to keep our baby, he became my protector and rescuer. On that day, he was my defender. And let me mention, I realize how very blessed I was to have a guy like Bruce in my life. I made a choice not to have an abortion, and he not only supported my decision but walked alongside me. Bruce's courage gave me the confidence and strength I needed to face an unplanned teenage pregnancy. But on that particular day, I had placed Bruce on a pedestal above God.

One day we were having a heated conversation, and I remember thinking, *What in the world am I doing? Why am I putting Bruce before God?* The Holy Spirit revealed to me that I was allowing Bruce to fill an area of my life that only God should fill. God needed to be my first love. I remember saying to Bruce after our argument, "That's it. You cannot be my number one any longer. God has to fill those areas you can't!" Bruce replied, "Praise the Lord! I need you to take the pressure off of me so that God can fill that space for you."

I had elevated Bruce above God, but I was now drawing a line in the sand, declaring God as my first love. Moving out of our home and leaving Bruce was a painful season, but I am thankful that through that experience I found the freedom to release the pressure I had put on him—pressure of trying to fill a place in my life that he was never supposed to fill.

By taking responsibility for myself, I also had to learn how to forgive. Bitterness had become such a stronghold in

> **I WAS STILL A VICTIM AND STILL HURTING, WHILE THE ABUSERS WERE MOVING ON WITH THEIR LIVES.**

my life that laying it down was very hard. It wasn't a coincidence that the two periods in my life that I misused alcohol, sexual abuse was the motivator for both. The first was after my rape and the second was after the sexual abuse in my neighborhood. I had turned to alcohol and drugs to numb my pain, but my aha moment with God taught me that my bitterness was like me drinking poison and hoping the other person would die. I was allowing the evil actions of others to continue to have control over my life. However, no one was getting hurt except me. I was still a victim and still hurting, while the abusers were moving on with their lives. I had to make a decision: Do I want to stay stuck in anger and bitterness, or do I want to take control of my life? Once that aha moment clicked, I found tremendous freedom, and I allowed forgiveness to grab hold of my heart.

One day I came upon Lamentations 3:55–59:

> I called on your name, LORD, from the depths of my pit. You heard my plea: "Do not close your ears to my cry for relief." You came near when I called you, and you said, "Do not fear." You, Lord, took up my case; you redeemed my life. LORD, you have seen the wrong done to me. Uphold my cause!

Those verses impacted me with such a revelation. I was in a bottomless pit, but God heard my cry. He came near to me, and I found his redemption.

During this time, Henry was due back in court for violating his probation terms. I had attended every court appearance during the trial and been following the case closely, and I planned to go to the hearing. But something changed inside of me. I realized through those Scripture verses that

God took up that case, and I had to surrender my hate and bitterness and get out of God's way. God was in control now, and he was upholding my cause. I had no desire to attend the hearing. I never went back again.

God had given me new eyes to forgive, not only Henry but even my rapist. I couldn't imagine being able to do that —to actually forgive. But it was a testimony of how much God had changed my heart. I had wanted to murder Henry and was filled with hatred for him, yet God gave me new eyes to see a lost man who desperately needed Jesus Christ. No one is beyond God's mercy and redemption. Only God could do that in my life. Only God!

ADULT AND TEEN CHALLENGE

As God was healing and transforming my life, I began to develop a burden to help people who were hurting and in crisis. I wanted to share my testimony of the saving power of Jesus Christ that had brought me freedom. It was no coincidence that God led Bruce and me to a ministry called Adult and Teen Challenge in northern Indiana, where we lived. We didn't know much about the organization except that it was a faith-based drug rehabilitation center. The program in our area was for men, but Adult and Teen Challenge centers are located throughout the United States and worldwide for men and women of all ages. Formerly known as Teen Challenge, the ministry was founded in 1958 by Reverend David Wilkerson in New York City. Its purpose is to reach those struggling with drug and alcohol addictions by offering them the same saving power I experienced in my life—the gospel of Jesus Christ.

Bruce was the first to be introduced to the Teen Challenge ministry. He went on a mission trip to Mexico through Nappanee Missionary Church, where we attend. Nappanee is the home church for Adult and Teen Challenge while the men go through the program. Bruce found out that three students and one staff member from the center would be on the mission trip with him. "I knew very little about Adult and Teen Challenge except that it was a drug rehab program," Bruce recalled. "I questioned why the rehab students were going on a mission trip and wondered, *Would I have to 'babysit' those delinquents?*"

While on that trip, Bruce quickly began to realize those "delinquents" were men growing in their relationship with Jesus Christ: "I remember sitting in the back of a truck driving from one site to another with the Teen Challenge guys and talking about life with them. They shared their testimonies with me, and we prayed together. What impressed me the most was all the Scriptures they had memorized. God blessed me through the experience of getting to know them, and I formed lasting friendships with several of them."

When they returned from that trip, the men in the program sang this beautiful, slightly off-key song at church on Sunday morning. As I listened, the song stirred so much emotion in me. They were singing about their redemption and it just spoke to me. From that day on, we started attending the Friday night chapel services at Adult and Teen Challenge.

We were both drawn by the presence of the Holy Spirit that we experienced during their chapel time. We met people who had struggles just like us. They had junk from their past, and many, like me, had been through a deep pit. There is total transparency at Teen Challenge that sometimes is difficult to find in a regular church setting. Everyone was there —masks off—loving and praising Jesus amid their recovery. It's this Jesus factor of the program that is undeniable when you walk through the doors.

Andy Collins, the director of the program, describes the Jesus factor based on Psalm 34:18: "The Lord is close to the brokenhearted and saves those who are crushed in spirit." At Adult and Teen Challenge, there is something special about the presence of God surrounding the broken and filling up the room. "Many of the men are raw in worshiping Jesus," Andy explains. "They have encountered the presence of God —many for the first time. Some of these men had needles in their arms a week ago or were in a jail cell months before. But in this structured environment, they are experiencing the grace and beauty of God for the first time. Their excitement for Jesus is contagious."

It was inspiring to be in an environment where no one was hiding their pain behind a mask. If I was struggling, I could go to someone and say, "I am not doing so well today." And there were always people willing to help me because they understood that struggle even as followers of Christ. Adult and Teen Challenge gave Bruce and me a sense of accountability, both in our marriage and in our relationship with God.

Bruce credits the program for giving him a greater understanding of the transformational work of Jesus Christ and helping him grow personally by walking a more Spirit-filled life. "Before meeting the men at the center, I knew I was a Christian and that Jesus had forgiven my sins. But I felt that my sins were not as bad as a Teen Challenge student," Bruce shared. "I remember singing praise songs with the men in the program and seeing the students raise their hands in worship. I thought they had more reason to praise the Lord than I did. I now know that was a lie and that my pride had held me back from really feeling the Savior's love."

God continued to give both me and Bruce new eyes for hurting people. I began to join Adult and Teen Challenge staff and students in street ministry. We would pray with and minister to prostitutes, meth addicts, alcoholics, and those hurting who needed to hear about the saving power of Jesus Christ. My heart softened toward those out on the street who had addictions, because I saw myself in their struggles.

ADULT AND TEEN CHALLENGE GAVE BRUCE AND ME A SENSE OF ACCOUNTABILITY, BOTH IN OUR MARRIAGE AND WITH GOD.

I am thankful that the ministry of Adult and Teen Challenge became a part of our lives. They have had a significant impact on my healing and my faith. We have made lasting friendships and are honored to step on as board members. It's hard to explain my love for Northern Indiana Adult and Teen Challenge, but when you experience it, there's nothing like the Teen Challenge family.

CHAPTER NINE

My Redemption Story

You, Lord, are forgiving and good,
abounding in love to all who call to you.
—PSALM 86:5

Taking responsibility for my healing was changing me from the inside out. I had been living in bitterness, but when I allowed God to transform my life, I began to experience real change within me, my marriage, and my family. But it took time to heal from the damage I had caused while I was living in my brokenness. I had hurt people badly, and like my wounds, it took time for them to heal too.

People were watching me, making sure I was the real deal and rightfully so. I knew they loved me, but they were guarded. Those cautious feelings began to lessen the more healing took place. My kids started to witness that I was not the same person. Bruce and I are thankful for how God restored our story, even as hard as it was to experience. If we did not walk through the hard stuff, we would not be where we are today. Because God transformed our hearts and lives, we were able to celebrate some beautiful moments with our family.

FAMILY TREE

One of those moments was our daughter's wedding day. Cassie was married in May 2015. On her wedding day, both sets of parents circled our daughter and son-in-law, and we prayed over them. It was a beautiful occasion for all of us, but I felt incredibly blessed to be there by Bruce's side on our daughter's special day.

Cassie had wanted to be married outdoors, but on the morning of their wedding, it started to rain. It was an unrelenting downpour throughout the day. Cassie's ceremony was scheduled for five o'clock, and as that time drew closer, there was still not a break in the clouds. We decided to move the ceremony indoors to a barn on the property. The barn had a metal roof, and while the rain poured down, it made it very difficult to hear anything inside. The only thing we could hear was the overwhelming clanging of the rain against the metal roof.

My father-in-law, who was performing their ceremony, said we would have to postpone the wedding until the rain stopped. I could see the disappointment in Cassie's eyes. All the planning and excitement of this day was interrupted by the non-stop torrential rain. We immediately began to pray. Suddenly, there was a break from the rain at five o'clock— the exact time of the ceremony! We were overjoyed that our prayers were answered.

Cassie looked stunningly beautiful in her wedding dress. She was married by her Grandpa Dyksen and our friend Chuck

Taylor, who took Cassie and me in after she was born. I had dreamed about my daughter's wedding since she was just a little girl, and I cherished being a part of her special day surrounded by friends and family. As soon as the ceremony ended, the rain began again. We knew God had shown his love to us, even in the little detail of allowing Cassie to get married on time.

Another memorable family event was helping our son, Carter, pull off a surprise engagement to his girlfriend—now our beautiful daughter-in-law—in the back of our church. After his surprise, both sides of the family met at a local coffee shop to celebrate, and we surrounded the couple and prayed over them.

> BECAUSE GOD TRANSFORMED OUR HEARTS AND LIVES, WE WERE ABLE TO CELEBRATE SOME BEAUTIFUL MOMENTS WITH OUR FAMILY.

There were so many special moments during Carter's wedding. His Aunt Rene lives out of town, but she was able to come and help set everything up on their wedding day. It was such a blessing to watch her jump into action to bless the kids and make their ceremony perfect. Both Carter and our daughter-in-law were incredibly nervous that day. They wanted to be close to each other before the ceremony to calm their nerves. They stood hand-in-hand in prayer—separated by a door so that they couldn't see each other. It was a beautiful moment captured in a photo, and one that, as a mother, I will always cherish remembering my son's wedding.

One spring day in 2018, we had a family lunch at Bruce's parents' house. Cassie and our son-in-law invited us to their apartment for dessert. While we were there, they handed us some Easter eggs. We opened them up and found a surprise—a baby announcement! Bruce and I were so happy to receive their baby news.

Several months later, we hosted a party to reveal the baby's gender. We invited about thirty people, including Cassie's in-laws. My son-in-law, a hunter, had a box filled with either pink or blue gun powder. He then shot the case, and out came pink gun powder. It was a girl! One of the photos from that day is pink gun powder in the shape of a heart. We were so excited to share the news. We were going to have our first grandchild—a baby girl!

Ever since the Lord pulled me out of my pit, I see hearts all over the place. It's like God is reminding me of his love for me. I know had I not healed from my brokenness, my kids would have still gotten married. They would have had their wedding ceremonies, but the difference is I was able to be there and witness all the memorable events. Our family tree was growing, and by God's grace, I got to experience all of it.

In December 2018, God blessed our family with a beautiful, healthy baby girl named Brinley. She looks so much like her mother, and she reminds us every day of how very different our family would have looked if we had not chosen life for our daughter, Cassie. Brinley brings us so much joy and laughter and is a constant reminder of God's love. As I write this with joyful tears, Exodus 15:13 comes to mind: "In your unfailing love you will lead the people you have redeemed. In your strength you will guide them to your holy dwelling." Brinley is a reflection of God's unfailing love to me and my family.

UNPLANNED

God revealed his faithfulness to me with each added blessing to our family tree. Our kids were happy and healthy, and we couldn't have asked for better spouses for each of them. Our son-in-law and our daughter-in-law fit perfectly into our family, and we get along with their parents and extended families. It was just one more gift God gave to me despite my dysfunctional family upbringing and continued strained relationship with my parents. I was finally settling into a good place in my life, and I felt like I was on the upswing of my redemption story.

I was actively involved in ministry opportunities sharing the gospel of Jesus Christ out on the streets, in jails, and volunteering alongside Adult and Teen Challenge. I was also working at the Prayerline, a prayer ministry where people around the world could call in for prayer. For eight-hour shifts, I would answer the phone and pray with people. This was my comfort zone. Ministry seemed to run in my veins, and God was developing my gifts through all these opportunities.

One day, I got a text that we had a Prayerline staff meeting on Saturday. At the meeting, the whole ministry received the news that they would be outsourcing to a call center. I was devastated. What would I do now? Where would I work?

Then one day, God spoke to me very clearly in a place I would have never expected—a movie theater. I quickly skimmed over a Facebook post by a friend recommending a film called *Unplanned*. I had no idea what the movie was about or that it was a true story and was based on a book. All I knew was that it was a faith-based film similar to *God's Not Dead* or *Facing the Giants*. Bruce and I hardly ever go out to movies, but if there is one that we know has a Christian message, we'll go out to support it in the theaters.

As we got comfortable in our theater seats and the movie began, I quickly realized this faith-based movie was not what I had expected at all. One of the opening scenes shows the character Abby Johnson, a Planned Parenthood clinic director, holding an ultrasound monitor on a woman's belly. She watches in horror, eyes transfixed on the monitor, as the doctor performs an abortion. Abby suddenly comes to terms with the violent reality of abortion as the image of a tiny, wiggly baby visible on the ultrasound screen just moments before suddenly disappears into a loud vacuum-like machine.

There I was suddenly captivated by a storyline that was like watching my life unfold before my eyes. I sat there stunned. It was a gut-wrenching reminder of my abortion. Even the beginning lines of the movie resonated with me when Abby Johnson says, "My story isn't an easy one to hear. I think I probably ought to warn you of that upfront." The movie then reveals Abby's life story from a college volunteer at an abortion clinic to eventually a director of Planned Parenthood—the largest abortion provider in America. When Abby comes face-to-face with the horrific reality of abortion in that procedure room, she decides she has to leave the abortion industry.

Nothing about that movie was easy for me to watch, but I am grateful that Abby Johnson stepped out in faith beyond the walls of Planned Parenthood and speaks out today about the atrocity of abortion. She is a strong pro-life advocate who not only courageously uses her life story to speak out against an industry that murders thousands of unborn babies a day, but she uses her post-abortive testimony to bring healing to women and men. She shares a tragic reality that I have experienced in my life: that women are hurt—physically, mentally, emotionally—inside the walls of abortion clinics.

As the credits began to scroll on the movie screen, and the audience sat in complete silence, I felt the overwhelming presence of the Holy Spirit speak to me. I knew right there in that theater that it was time to tell the rest of my story. I had been open about my past sexual abuse in counseling. So much healing had taken place in my life, but there was one area where I was not willing to go. I knew that sharing my abortion story would involve another level of shame, guilt, and trauma. I had locked that painful experience away in a vault, but *Unplanned* opened that area of my heart. It was as if God was gently prompting me to step out in faith and share my story too. Looking back, I realize he was directing me to a new ministry. God had closed the Prayerline ministry because he had another plan for me. God knew I was ready, but in his divine providence, he also knew it would lead me to more healing.

THE WHOLE STORY

Though I knew the Holy Spirit was directing me to tell my story, I didn't know when or how to share it. God was prompting me to step out, but there was no clear road map. One Friday night after attending chapel at Adult and Teen Challenge, I planned a testimony night with a group of women connected with the ministry. We ordered pizza and met together in one of their living rooms for a time to share our testimonies.

We all sat around looking at each other, wondering who would break the ice by sharing their testimony first. It was an awkward but funny moment. I was hesitant to share my testimony and didn't want to be the first one. So one person in the group spoke up to share first, and then some of the women directed the conversation to me: "You coordinated this, Serena, so you have to tell your story." I agreed, knowing full well I was responsible for gathering everyone together. But I was nervous, not only about sharing my testimony but about revealing the *whole* story.

> IT WAS TIME TO SHARE GOD'S REDEMPTION AND GRACE IN MY LIFE WITH A BROADER AUDIENCE AND FOR A BIGGER PURPOSE.

I was stunned that I could even get the words out. I started from the beginning, and I opened up about the entire timeline of my life. It was the first time I had shared about my abortion since I told Bruce as a teenager. There it was. I opened the painful vault, and it was out. In response, there was no judgment, only love and compassion by everyone in the room. When I finished, my friend turned to me and said, "Serena, you have to share this story. Now is the time." I knew what she meant. It was time to share God's redemption and grace in my life with a broader audience and for a bigger purpose. "I know," I responded. "But how?"

My friend urged me to type out my testimony, and she had a friend edit it for me. Though I was sure I was supposed to share my story with a pro-life organization, I wasn't familiar with any and didn't know who to contact. I had little knowledge of the pro-life movement but I was ready to share my abortion story to help other women.

God was not only prompting me to tell my story, but he was stirring my heart to reach out to women at abortion clinics. My heart has always been to help people. I loved being a part of the Prayerline, street ministry, and sharing about Jesus with drug addicts, pimps, prostitutes, and anyone who is down and out. But I knew that God was now directing me to minister outside of abortion clinics.

I didn't know where to begin. The first organization I came across was St. Joseph County Right to Life. Their name intrigued me, so I looked them up. They sounded like a great organization as I read about their mission to protect all of human life from fertilization to natural death. I was particularly drawn to the words stating that the organization "saves children, women, and men from the devastating effects of abortion."[6] So I sent them my story, and I asked if they ever minister to women outside of abortion clinics. They said they did, and in fact an unlicensed abortion clinic called Whole Woman's Health was about to open up in South Bend, Indiana. Right to Life was training counselors to minister to the women at the clinic, and they asked if I would like to sign up to become a licensed sidewalk counselor. I responded with a firm, "Yes—sign me up!"

At this time, a writer connected with me and asked if she could share my testimony on her blog site. I agreed, and she told me that sometimes her blog posts get picked up by other news outlets and asked permission to share my story with other sites. I agreed, not knowing what to expect. It was one thing to share my story with family, in a living room with trusted friends, or with a local pro-life organization, but sharing it with the outside world was a bit scary.

I knew I was to be obedient and share my testimony no matter what the response might be. My story eventually made it to a few pro-life news outlets, and suddenly it seemed every time I opened my social media accounts, I saw my shared article. I began to get one message after another from people thanking me for sharing my abortion story. I was amazed at all the responses! For weeks, I would get individuals and media sites asking if they could share my story. I had told my whole story out of obedience, and God was faithfully using it. Through the process, I began to see the hand of God, and he was directing me all along the way.

POST-ABORTION HEALING

While my story began to circulate on various news outlets, I attended the sidewalk counseling training at Right to Life. During a break between training sessions, I began to chat with one of the seasoned sidewalk counselors who leads abortion recovery classes. I told her about watching the movie *Unplanned* and how I felt God was leading me to share my story. She was so kind and asked me, "Have you ever attended an abortion recovery retreat to get healing for your abortion?" I remember smiling, but honestly, I think I might have rolled my eyes a bit at her suggestion. With all the counseling

I had been through, I felt I was at a good place in my recovery. I didn't think I needed post-abortive healing. I politely took her business card figuring I might share it with other women who could use it.

After completing my training, I began sidewalk counseling outside of Whole Woman's Health abortion clinic. I noticed the clinic offered "VIP abortion care" to their patients. This was a private abortion appointment with no other patients in the office. They even offered an after-abortion care basket. They framed the whole abortion appointment as if it was a day at the spa. I couldn't believe it. What they were offering was not VIP care at all. I began praying about what to do. I felt the Lord leading me to make the women feel special, like a VIP, before they even walked into the doors of the clinic. I decided to put together gift bags with small items for each mom.

I wanted to include life-affirming literature in each gift bag, so I reached out to my local pregnancy clinic called RETA (Reason Enough To Act). They are a faith-based, pregnancy clinic and family resource center offering services to women facing unplanned pregnancies. I met with the Pregnancy Loss Support Coordinator about providing literature for the bags. She also invited me to the next abortion recovery retreat they were having. It was coming up quickly, so I immediately decided to attend. I signed up for their abortion recovery Bible study called *Forgiven and Set Free*.[7] It is typically a twelve-week Bible study series, but they offered it as a weekend session, which was a rare event.

My purpose in attending the Bible study was to learn how to help other post-abortive women. There was no doubt God was opening doors for me as I shared my story, and as I ministered outside of Whole Woman's Health abortion clinic, other women were reaching out to me with their abortion stories. They were hurting and needed proper direction for their healing. I soon realized that the abortion recovery ministry was a vital component of the healing process. I couldn't recommend it to others if I wasn't willing to do it myself.

But that weekend became more about what I needed in my own personal recovery. It was the last piece of my healing puzzle—healing through Scripture that focused specifically on my abortion. There was a reason that I allowed my abortion to be the final point of my healing: abortion brings up feelings of grief, loss, and regret. I had lived with this grief all my life, thinking there was no forgiveness for it, so I locked it away.

Abortion becomes the secret that no one talks about. Some women choose abortion, but many have the decision made for them. There is story after story of women who suffer from the effects of an abortion that they didn't choose. But it doesn't matter how they arrived behind the walls of an abortion clinic; what matters is the trauma they experienced because of that abortion. Women and men live with that trauma every day—sometimes for many, many years—and they need healing.

As I searched each Scripture verse, I was reminded of how much my heavenly Father loved me and wanted to heal all my busted, broken pieces. God sent his Son to die on the cross to heal my wounds and make me whole again. There is forgiveness for abortion through the saving power of Jesus Christ.

The greatest lie Satan speaks into the lives of those who have experienced abortion is that God will not forgive you. I carried that lie for so many years. First John 1:9 says, "If we confess our sins, he is faithful and just and will forgive us our sins and purify us from all unrighteousness." It doesn't say he will forgive *some* of our sins. No, he forgives *all* our sins and purifies us—makes us clean and sets us free. I had to learn how to walk in that freedom so I could forgive myself.

ELLIANA GRACE

Finding freedom from my abortion involved realizing there was no more condemnation. The Bible study was not only directing me to walk in God's forgiveness, but it was allowing me to grieve the loss of my child. The most powerful part of the study was when it talked about naming my baby. It was time to bring my grief into focus. I began to pray and ask God to give me a glimpse of my child.

In my time of prayer, I had this beautiful vision of a young lady with long, dark hair standing beside a young man with blonde hair. They were standing side by side smiling, and it felt as if they were both cheering me on. I sensed that the young lady was my aborted child, and the young man was our son whom we miscarried. I know it might sound a bit crazy, but I believe God gave me that gift of allowing me that beautiful moment to experience their presence. That vision brought healing and allowed me to mourn the loss of my two children.

I felt the Lord leading me to name my daughter Elliana Grace. The name Elliana means "my God has answered" and Grace means "kindness, mercy, and favor." I began weeping when I realized the significance of both words. That's precisely what God had done in my life: he answered me with grace, and his kindness was overflowing in my life.

During the retreat, I called Bruce and shared with him that God had shown me that our miscarried baby was a boy. We had never mourned the loss of our baby individually or as a couple. I asked Bruce to name our son, and he gave him the name Malachi, which means "messenger." It was a fitting name considering our story is a message of hope and healing.

I left the retreat feeling like my family was now complete. We added two names to our family tree, and the vision and names of my children restored dignity to their identity. I was able to grieve and mourn the loss of my two babies. I was allowed to speak their names and be their mother.

Forgiven and Set Free allowed me to step out in freedom from my abortion. I returned home from that weekend with the promise of Scripture: "You, Lord, are forgiving and good, abounding in love to all who call to you" (Psalm 86:5). I am so grateful for those who directed me to the abortion healing ministry. Sometimes others can see things that we can't. I was blind to the understanding that I needed abortion healing. It not only healed my deep emotional scars, but it made me realize that was the process I needed to go through to be able to continue to share my story. There is hope and healing after abortion.

CHAPTER TEN

Beauty for Ashes

He has sent me to bind up the brokenhearted,
to proclaim freedom for the captives and
release from darkness for the prisoners.
—Isaiah 61:1

A s I began to walk in obedience to the Holy Spirit's prompting to share my story, I witnessed the hand of God guiding me. He was preparing me for a mission. More doors were opening to share my testimony, and the abortion recovery retreat was perfectly timed for the path God was leading me on. Had I not said yes to that weekend healing opportunity, I would not have been ready for the bigger purpose he had for me. He prepared me mentally, emotionally, and spiritually for what was coming. I am so grateful because I could have never predicted the next door God would call me to walk through.

DAY OF REMEMBRANCE

The *Forgiven and Set Free* study provided me with personal healing and a better understanding of how to minister to post-abortive mothers and fathers. One day, the Lord laid it on my heart to have a special healing service for parents to grieve the loss of their aborted babies. I had no idea how to schedule this type of service, but I wanted to obey what God was asking me to do.

I felt that the healing service should be on September 14, 2019, and it should be held outside of the Whole Woman's Health abortion clinic. I was so new to the pro-life movement I didn't realize that every September several pro-life organizations co-sponsor an annual National Day of Remembrance for Aborted Children. When I reached out to Right to Life and told them about the memorial service I was planning, they connected me with Eric Scheidler, the Executive Director of the Pro-Life Action League.[8] Eric is from a family that has been actively involved in the pro-life movement since shortly after the Supreme Court's *Roe v. Wade* decision in 1973. His father and mother, Joe and Ann Scheidler, founded the League in 1980 to recruit and equip

> THE LORD LAID IT ON MY HEART TO HAVE A SPECIAL HEALING SERVICE FOR PARENTS TO GRIEVE THE LOSS OF THEIR ABORTED BABIES.

pro-life leaders to save babies from abortion in their communities.

I emailed Eric about the event I was planning, and he replied that memorial services for aborted children typically are not held at abortion clinic sites because they will inevitably look more like an abortion protest than a prayer service. However, since Whole Woman's Health facility was featured regularly on the news—because it was an unlicensed abortion clinic that was allowed to operate in Indiana—Eric thought it might be appropriate for what I wanted to accomplish.

With the date and location in place, I began to call abortion recovery ministries to invite any women or men who had gone through post-abortive healing to attend the memorial service. I learned how important it was for those who would attend to have completed an abortion recovery process due to the emotions involved in this type of event.

At one point while planning the prayer memorial, I felt overwhelmed and decided to cancel it. *What was I doing?* I realized the seriousness of this type of occasion and questioned whether I had correctly heard the Lord's directions for me. After much prayer, I felt a peace about the event and decided to go through with the plans. Several abortion recovery ministries reached out to women who they thought were ready to attend a Day of Remembrance memorial, and four of them signed up.

One afternoon, three of the ladies came over to my house, and we sat around my kitchen table, making posters with our children's names on them. We decorated them with markers and meaningful messages to honor each child. I painted mine with bright, colorful letters: *My choice has a name, Elliana Grace. Forever in my heart. Love, Your Mom.* It was comforting to gather with other women who had lost their children to abortion and prepare for a Day of Remembrance. We had all walked through biblical repentance, forgiveness, and healing over abortion. Society claims abortion is a choice, but walking through post-abortive healing allowed us to properly mourn and remember that "choice" has a name. Our posters were visual representations of the names of our children. We were mothers grieving the loss of each child lost to abortion.

The prayer memorial was scheduled for Saturday, at nine o'clock in the morning. The whole week before the service, I made sure to cover the event in prayer each day. On Friday, I purposely stayed off social media to spend more time in prayer. My friend from Right to Life messaged me that we needed to pray about what was happening regarding the Dr. George Klopfer news. Her message piqued my curiosity. I knew that name for several reasons. Dr. Ulrich (George) Klopfer had recently been in the news because he was an Indiana abortion doctor who had passed away just days before on September 3. But I also knew his name because I had done preliminary research on my abortion, and Dr. Klopfer was linked to the location of my abortion at the Women's Pavilion in South Bend.

HEADLINES

Friday night before I went to bed, I decided to check Face-book. I quickly flipped through my newsfeed and read the headline: "Breaking: Thousands of fetal remains found in the home of former South Bend abortion doctor." I paused and gasped. The photo linked to the headlines grabbed my attention. Dr. Klopfer's photo brought back instant memories. I remembered his face, his hair, his glasses. There was even a photo of him smiling, and I felt this queasy feeling in my stomach. Dr. Klopfer was the man who had performed my abortion when I was thirteen years old; there was no doubt about it. The news was horrifying. Indiana authorities had found over 2,200 fetal remains—babies—on the property of his home in Illinois. His family made the gruesome discovery while going through his personal belongings after his death.

I crawled into bed, completely shocked by the news. My whole body went numb, and I began crying uncontrollably. Here I was, about to lead a memorial service—the very next day—with other post-abortive mothers, to mourn and remember my daughter Elliana Grace. Now I read the news that the abortion doctor who aborted my child had thousands of baby remains at his house. I cried out to God, "Is my daughter one of those babies?" I couldn't shake the horrific images in my head. My tears turned to anger over the abortion industry and even the Whole Woman's Health clinic that was allowed to operate without a state license. If Dr. Klopfer took baby remains from his licensed clinics, what was happening behind the walls of an unlicensed clinic?

As I lay in bed with tears streaming down my face, praying, and asking for answers, I suddenly felt the overwhelming peace of God. This supernatural calm came over me, and the Lord reminded me that even if the body of Elliana Grace was one of those 2,200 babies, her soul was safe in God's loving arms. I had nothing to fear. My heavenly Father was holding all those babies. God was not surprised by this news. And then, just like that, I understood the timing behind why God directed me to lead a Day of Remembrance for aborted children on Saturday, September 14, 2019—the very day after Dr. Klopfer made the headlines. God knew post-abortive mothers and fathers, like myself, would see the news and feel the intense pain of abortion all over again. But our heavenly Father loves us so much that he provided a place and time of healing during the tragic news in our community.

The next morning it was a bright, sunny day. We had a beautiful prayer memorial in front of the unlicensed abortion clinic, Whole Woman's Health. An Adult and Teen Challenge staff member was the lead pastor for the service. Several people from the community joined the memorial as well. The abortion clinic is located on a busy street in South Bend, Indiana. Our group reverently gathered in a circle on a grassy area between the road and the building. Several of us shared our abortion stories, and the pastor led us in prayer. Three of us with signs stood in front of the clinic displaying our babies' names on our posters. We stood there solemnly —not in protest but remembrance—mourning the loss of our children. But we also remembered those 2,200 babies who were denied the gift of life. I was in awe of God's timing. We were a small gathering, but those traveling that busy road witnessed our Day of Remembrance for our aborted children with the abortion clinic as our backdrop, and as the horror of abortion continued to make headlines all across the country.

FOR SUCH A TIME AS THIS

Right away, I saw firsthand how the Klopfer news was affecting women and men in my community. While I was still at the clinic that day for the memorial, I began to talk with a post-abortive woman who was there to minister to women before they entered the abortion clinic. The news was affecting her emotionally, and she was having a difficult time. She began sobbing and sharing intimate details of her life that broke my heart. She then pointed to a gas line that had been dug out across the street from the clinic. "I know they are burying babies there," she cried. She was overwhelmed with trauma, and the headlines were opening deep wounds. I grabbed her hands and began to pray. She was a post-abortive woman who had not gone through healing. I realized why it was so critical that our memorial service include only those who had gone through

WE STOOD THERE SOLEMNLY—NOT IN PROTEST BUT REMEMBRANCE— MOURNING THE LOSS OF OUR CHILDREN.

abortion recovery. Had I invited women who had not walked through healing, the service would have looked very different that day.

As the Klopfer story unfolded and more details were revealed in the news, many hurting post-abortive mothers and fathers began to reach out to me. My inbox was flooded on my social media and email accounts. People shared their abortion stories with me and were dealing with those same intense feelings that I felt regarding the baby remains found at Dr. Klopfer's home. My community was hurting.

To those not touched by abortion, the news was merely about the questions surrounding Dr. Ulrich Klopfer. Why did he keep the thousands of baby remains in his garage? Did anyone else know that he was taking the bodily remains of his aborted victims? What kind of man was Dr. Klopfer? But for those of us who had experienced abortion, especially by the hands of Dr. Klopfer, our questions were painful to ponder. Not knowing if our baby was in one of those medical bags stuffed inside a box, we were haunted by the possibility. The news opened deep wounds for those who had not gone through proper healing.

I began to minister to those reaching out to me, and I realized I was walking through another door God had planned for me. It was by God's grace that he provided abortion healing for me so quickly back in August. Had I not gone through that healing process, I wouldn't have been prepared for the Klopfer headlines. God knew what I needed to experience so that I could use my story and healing to help others.

God had called me for such a time as this in my state of Indiana and my community. He was redeeming my story to help other women and men to heal and find forgiveness from abortion. Several days after the Klopfer story broke, I shared a Scripture from Isaiah 61 on my Facebook page:

> "He has sent me to bind up the brokenhearted, to proclaim freedom for the captives and release from darkness for the prisoners, to proclaim the year of the LORD's favor and the day of vengeance of our God, to comfort all who mourn, and provide for those who grieve in Zion—to bestow on them a crown of beauty instead of ashes, the oil of joy instead of mourn-

ing, and the garment of praise instead of a spirit of despair." (Isaiah 61:1–3)

I was living in the freedom that Isaiah speaks about, with a crown of beauty instead of ashes. My healing took time, but it was worth it. God's promise of grace and forgiveness is a beautiful covenant for those who believe in the name of Jesus Christ for our salvation. It cannot be broken or moved. God's mercy and truth hold us together, and he was using my victory to help others find that same kind of freedom. There were pain and heartbreak around me, but I felt the overwhelming presence of God in how he was using my story. All of it humbled me.

PRESS CONFERENCE

Several days after the Klopfer news began circulating, my community seemed to have more questions than answers. I was asked by both the Allen County and St. Joseph County Right to Life organizations to share my story at two press conferences. I chuckled to myself at their request. When I felt that God was asking me to share my story after I watched the movie *Unplanned*, I made a special request. I prayed, "God, I will do anything for you. I will willingly share my story, but please don't ask me to speak in front of a crowd." I laugh at that silly request now. If God called me to obey, I certainly couldn't put stipulations on my obedience.

The press conferences were held at two abortion clinics where Dr. Klopfer had performed abortions. One was in Fort Wayne, Indiana, and the other was where my abortion was performed—Women's Pavilion in South Bend. Not only was I to share my story publicly in front of the press with cameras, but I was to speak at the very place where my trauma took place. Again, God's timing of healing and recovery was sustaining me all along the way. I was nervous, but I knew I was ready.

The press was all too familiar with Dr. Ulrich (George) Klopfer over the years. His reputation preceded him before the news of his death and the horrific discovery at his home. Although he lived in Illinois, he performed abortions in Fort Wayne, Gary, and South Bend, Indiana. In 2014, Klopfer was charged with a misdemeanor for failure to file a public Termination of Pregnancy Report of an abortion performed on a thirteen-year-old patient. In Indiana, the law requires an abortionist to report an abortion performed on a child under age sixteen to the Department of Child Services and the Indiana Health Department within three days.

Dr. Klopfer and the Women's Pavilion were the sources of ongoing violations and injunctions over several years. Numerous complaints were brought against Klopfer in violating governing codes and laws in abortion recordkeeping. Jackie Appleman, Executive Director of St. Joseph Right to Life, heard multiple stories and complaints from women who had abortions by Dr. Klopfer. "There were ongoing complaints that Dr. Klopfer would botch abortions all the time. From cutting corners on providing sedation to patients, not making sure all the baby body parts were removed in a surgical procedure, to complaints of pain and complications after an abortion," Jackie noted. The *Journal Gazette* described him as "Indiana's most prolific abortion doctor in history,"[9] performing tens of thousands of abortions over several decades. In 2016, the Women's Pavilion closed its doors, and the Indiana Medical Licensing Board suspended Dr. Ulrich Klopfer's medical license.

Of course, in 2016, I was unaware of any of this information regarding Dr. Klopfer. But the recent revelations about the man helped me to understand the horrific circumstances regarding my abortion at age thirteen. While I was going through post-abortive healing, I often battled with spiritual warfare. The lie I kept hearing was that I was making it all up in my head. *You are a liar. You never had an abortion.* Those thoughts plagued my mind. I was never so relieved to receive the court records that detailed my rape and abortion, as well as read the details about Dr. Klopfer in the news. Seeing his name and his face confirmed that I wasn't losing my mind. I prayed over the enemy's attack that was attempting to destroy the freedom I had found from my abuse and abortion.

I knew I was walking in freedom, but was I ready to share my story with the world at the press conferences? I will never forget how Cathie Humbarger, Executive Director of Allen County Right to Life, laid her hand on my shoulder and prayed for me before the first press conference began. That prayer was what I needed to calm my nerves. Cathie was the first to speak at the press conference. She relayed the news of the horrific discovery in Dr. Klopfer's garage and the history of his sloppy practices in the medical field. She ended her speech:

> These 2,246 lives speak to an abortion industry that cares nothing for human dignity and nothing for the women it alleges to help. These lives show that we can, and must, do better in recognizing the value in every human life. May God receive all the glory for whatever glory there is in this heartbreaking story. The people standing with me are part of this story, along with many others.[10]

Cathie's words resonated with my purpose in sharing my story. I knew that whatever came out of my mouth, I wanted God to get all the glory. My heartbreaking story was already redeemed. Dr. Ulrich Klopfer was a part of that story, and yes, I was a woman who horrifically lost her baby. But my purpose was to represent what God had done in my life. I stood behind that podium, a bit shaky but determined in my mission. I shared my story and ended the speech with my heart's calling: "I want to encourage post-abortive women and men not to hold on to turmoil any longer. Please reach out for help and healing. There are many people in the community who want to help you with your healing process. We are here for you. Just because you made a choice does not mean you deserve to sit in pain and suffering. There is forgiveness, hope, and healing for you."

> JUST BECAUSE YOU MADE A CHOICE DOES NOT MEAN YOU DESERVE TO SIT IN PAIN AND SUFFERING.

The next day I had another press conference at the closed Women's Pavilion in South Bend, the site of my abortion over thirty years before. It was difficult to give that speech again at the exact location where so much of my pain and heartbreak began, but I had so many friends and family praying for me, and I felt God's strength. After the press conference, I was able to have great conversations with many in the media. At times, I think the press was looking for someone who was a crying mess for a dramatic storyline. Several in the media questioned why I wasn't falling apart. That would open the door to share my faith and testimony. A reporter from one of the more prominent news outlets showed compassion to me and my story. I asked him if I could pray over him when we finished the interview. He responded, "I have never had anyone ask to pray for me before and do it." God would give me several opportunities to witness God's love and mercy, specifically with people in the media.

Later that evening, a friend tagged me in a photo on Facebook. It was a picture of me giving my speech at the press conference with the Women's Pavilion sign prominently displayed in the background on the wall of the abortion clinic. Her post read, "So proud of my dear friend for sharing about abortionist Ulrich Klopfer. Pray that lives are changed through her testimony. Choose life. Pray for justice to honor the unborn lives that were cut short before taking their first breath."

Only God could take the life of an abused thirteen-year-old girl, who experienced the tragedy of rape and abortion, and make her life a testimony of his grace—at the very location of that event in her life. They say a picture is worth a thousand words. That photo spoke volumes with God receiving all the glory.

2,411

About a month later, there was another grisly discovery. The authorities found more baby remains in the trunk of Dr. Klopfer's car located on a lot he owned. The total number of aborted babies found in Klopfer's possession was 2,411. Not only did investigators find the baby remains in various forms of decay, but they found hundreds of health records at both locations. A preliminary report by the office of Indiana Attorney General Curtis T. Hill Jr. noted that most of the baby remains and medical records appeared to be from Dr. Klopfer's medical practice during the years from 2000 to 2003. Investigators do not know why Klopfer would have kept the baby remains, and we are unlikely to ever know the reason after his death.

My community and the state of Indiana were significantly affected by the news surrounding the discovery of the remains of 2,411 babies. A tragic number but not nearly reflective of the approximately 862,320 lives lost to abortion each year in the United States.[11] The headlines shared all around the world forced everyone to pause and take into account the reality of abortion. The discoveries in Dr. Klopfer's vehicle and garage were not simply "clumps of cells" in medical bags. They were the tiny but recognizable bodies of unborn children. They were human lives—2,411 babies. They were sons, daughters, nieces, nephews, and grandchildren, each one uniquely made in the image of God.

A mass burial service was provided for the babies in a cemetery in South Bend. A funeral home donated the burial plot for a place to remember and give those precious babies a proper burial. Hundreds of single long-stemmed red roses were strewn across the fresh plot of dirt. A simple granite headstone marked the 2,411 precious unborn babies who were buried there. Nearly one hundred people attended the funeral on a cold and overcast day. I was asked to give brief remarks at the ceremony and was nervous, but I shared what was on my heart. I knew my words needed to focus on God's love for post-abortive mothers and fathers: "At the end of the day, no matter what the world is screaming, mothers and fathers of these children buried here today are hurting deeply," I shared. "These were their children, and it was a loss of life, and it hurts. I know for myself, God had given me a mother's heart, even at age thirteen. Thank you for allowing this to be a place for post-abortive mothers and fathers to mourn their children. Thank you for being a part of their healing process."

From my memorial service, the day after the Klopfer news story broke, to the day of the funeral service for the 2,411 babies, God was revealing he is there for the broken-hearted. He binds our wounds and sets the captives free. Although the headlines shocked me and forced me to re-member the physical and emotional pain of abortion, God was there with me. He provided the healing I needed to be the voice for those 2,411 voiceless babies. And he allowed me to minister to hurting mothers and fathers desperate to find freedom from the guilt and shame of abortion. I don't know why Dr. Ulrich Klopfer kept 2,411 aborted baby remains, but I watched in awe as God used those horrific headlines to bring healing to a hurting post-abortive community. What I know about my Jesus is he can take any tragic story and redeem it for his glory.

CHAPTER ELEVEN

Grace and Freedom

And we know that in all things God works
for the good of those who love him, who
have been called according to his purpose.
—ROMANS 8:28

More doors were continuing to open for me to share my story and in larger settings. It was only a matter of months from when I first shared my testimony with that small group of ladies in a living room until I was speaking in front of large groups and the media. I was invited to speak at banquets, churches, podcasts, news stations such as Fox News, and colleges. A large German news outlet even interviewed Bruce and me for a documentary on abortion. God was opening door after door, and it was all in his perfect timing.

There was some wariness as I began to share my story. I was walking in unchartered waters and it was overwhelming.

God was leading me to share my testimony but Bruce and I wanted to use wisdom in how it was shared. Early on, we met with our pastor about all these speaking opportunities. He cautioned us to watch out for those who might want to use my story for personal gain. We knew we had to put up safeguards regarding where and with whom I shared my testimony. It was a sensitive and controversial topic, but we knew that God was using it to bring healing to others. We had to be prayerful about which door to walk through and ensure that our focus was on God's redemption and grace. We have a sign above our door as we leave our house that reads "Matthew 4:19: Come follow me, Jesus said, and I will send you out to fish for people." My prayer, as I walk out my door, is that the focus not be on me but on what God has done. I want my story to be first and foremost a ministry—to offer healing and discipleship.

RAPE EXCEPTION

When I chose to act in obedience and publicly speak out about my abortion, I had no idea how it would help others to speak out as well. The huge lie in the abortion industry is that abortion is just a standard medical procedure and does not harm you. They cloak the procedure as "healthcare" claiming it is routine, healthy, and without side effects. Abortion clinics use deceptive language to normalize abortion so that a woman will think she can have her pregnancy terminated one day, and then life will go back to normal the next. This couldn't be further from the truth. On the day of my abortion, that procedure negatively affected me for the rest of my life. It took me years to not only understand this but confront it and find healing.

The more I shared about the pain I experienced from abortion, the more women and men began to reach out to me. My ongoing depression, my dysfunctional family relationships, the struggles in my marriage, my physical health problems, and my addiction struggles: other people were finding similarities in their stories and connecting it with their abortion too. When I chose to speak about my abortion transparently, it helped others to connect with their trauma, and I was able to help guide people to counseling and healing.

I am aware that my abortion story is different from many others. Not only did my abortion take place at the tender age of thirteen, but it was a result of rape. I am included in the 1 percent of women who abort because they are victims of rape.[12] The 1 percent "rape exception" is often used to justify all abortions. But to be transparent, it is important for people to understand that my abortion was worse than my rape. I have said this multiple times as I have publicly shared my story.

I certainly don't want people to misunderstand me. My rape was devastating. It was a trauma that took away my innocence and robbed me of peace. Rape gave me mental flashbacks that paralyzed me with fear. There were days that I could not scrub my skin hard enough to feel clean from the ugliness of sexual abuse. Rape was an act of violence done to me. But abortion is also an act of violence. When I was old enough to understand what abortion was and how it purposely took another life, it devastated me. I would never purposely take another life. That's not who I am. That's not who my parents are or most women I talk to who have had an abortion.

On the day of my abortion appointment, I was taken to a counseling room. When I think of counseling now, I think of help and something that is going to further my healing, not cause more damage. I was lied to. They never once told me a baby was growing inside of me. I would never hurt an innocent baby. The abortion clinic never mentioned my rape or offered my parents help for the trauma of my sexual abuse. Instead, it was just trauma after trauma, which resulted in even more trauma. What dignity I had left was ripped out of me. I was treated like trash. They didn't care that I was a child who had been raped. Even if the clinic thought they were "helping" me, you don't yell at a young patient on a table and send her home a bloody mess. Abortion is not healthcare, no matter how they package it. It might be a Band-Aid idea before you enter the clinic, but once you have that abortion, your life will never be the same. Performing an abortion on a woman after rape is like putting a bandage on a gunshot wound. It will never fix it.

Satan made abortion seem like the best answer to my situation. I am sure my parents had a million thoughts running through their heads, and without a firm foundation in Christ, what else did they have to stand on? All they knew was fear, guilt, shame, uncertainty, and unhealed trauma in their lives. I have had people ask me, "Why would you have wanted to keep the rapist's baby?" You don't heal a victim of sexual abuse and rape by inflicting more abuse and violence. Abortion left me empty and traumatized, and it took the life of an innocent baby—my baby. Abortion left a gaping hole in our hearts that changed my family forever. Once the abortion was done, it was final. There was no turning back.

If I was going to talk about my abortion, I had to honestly convey how abortion emotionally and physically damaged me more than my rape. There was no way around it. If rape is the exception for abortion, then why did abortion leave me in more pain? Rape and abortion are both acts of violence, without exception.

SILENT NO MORE

On January 24, 2020, I had the opportunity to share my testimony on the steps of the United States Supreme Court while attending the National March for Life in Washington, DC. Three friends and I all attended the march to share our abortion regret stories, and we walked with the Silent No More Awareness organization. Silent No More is a campaign "whereby Christians make the public aware of the devastation abortion brings to women and men. The campaign seeks to expose and heal the secrecy and silence surrounding the emotional and physical pain of abortion."[13]

It was my first time attending the March for Life. I walked among thousands and thousands of people from all across the United States, all united for one cause: to give a voice to the unborn. The Silent No More group helped to lead the marchers toward the steps of the Supreme Court. Many of us were holding signs that read "I Regret My Abortion" or "Women Do Regret Abortion." As we walked along Constitution Avenue among the throngs of marchers, women would come up to us and whisper in our ears, "Me too," or "You are the heroes—thank you." We heard that over and over again as we marched.

The march ends at the steps of the Supreme Court. On the base of the steps was a small Silent No More podium with a microphone. Nearly forty of us were ready to share our abortion regret stories in front of thousands of marchers. We were met by some pro-abortion protesters who stood in front of the podium yelling and trying to silence us. We patiently waited for them to settle down, and many of us started to pray for these women. Eventually, we were able to take turns stepping up to the podium, each sharing our pain from abortion. We all shared different stories but with the same theme of loss and regret. We mourned the loss of our children and testified that the only thing that healed us and set us free was Jesus Christ and abortion healing.

When it was my turn to speak, I made my way to the podium, but I had to pause for a moment. A group of bagpipe players were still marching, and the music was very loud. I had to wait as they passed. It was a silly moment for me. There I was on the steps of the Supreme Court ready to speak to thousands of people, and I had to wait. A friend of mine who came to the march silently mouthed to me in the crowd, "Only you!" God has a sense of humor. I told God I didn't want to speak in public, and out of all those forty people, I had to wait to speak. I still chuckle at that moment.

When things settled down, I shared my abortion regret story and ended with these words: "Today I stand here and ask that you remember my story. God gave this thirteen-year-old, raped girl a mother's heart. Abortion hurts women. It doesn't matter the age or the situation. And this is why I am silent no more!"

I was in awe of where God had allowed me to share my story. I was able to speak on the steps of the United States Supreme Court, where forty-seven years earlier *Roe v. Wade* tragically made it legal in our country to kill unborn children. But that is what God can do when you step out in obedience —he turns your story into his redemption testimony on the steps of our nation's highest court.

When all the speakers from Silent No More were done, I asked my friend what stuck out most about each woman's story. She responded, "Each woman just needed one person." She was right. Women who go to abortion clinics are scared, and they are looking for help. Sometimes all it takes is just one person to reach out, walk alongside her, and help her choose life for her child.

SILENCE IN THE PEWS

After attending the *Forgiven and Set Free* retreat, I also attended two other retreats through the Deeper Still ministry. Deeper Still is an abortion recovery ministry that offers healing through weekend retreats. These events are wonderful healing sessions for both women and men who need to walk in freedom from their past abortion. I was able to attend Deeper Still both as an attendee and as a leader. I had no idea these ministries even existed until I trained to be a sidewalk counselor. I realized more and more people within the church had no idea about these abortion healing ministries either.

As God was using my story of post-abortive healing through my speaking opportunities and one-to-one conversations, I also felt him calling me to the church. Several weeks later, I was invited to lead a women's retreat with Northside Baptist Church in Elkhart, Indiana. I had previously shared my testimony with their congregation on a Sunday morning. The pastor's wife reached out to me and asked if I would be willing to speak at their annual women's retreat. As more doors were opening to share my story, I felt God laying it on my heart to see both women and men in the church find healing from abortion.

The theme of the women's retreat that weekend was Unshakeable. On the first night, I was asked to share my story for about forty minutes. I began telling my story, and all of a sudden, I felt the Holy Spirit wanted me to end early and just stop. It felt weird. I didn't know why, but I quickly wrapped up the session with prayer.

After abruptly ending my speaking, I began casually talking with a couple of ladies. Someone interrupted our conversation and said I was needed in another room. I went to a back room where a woman was crying. She was upset, and she wanted to go home. "I don't think I can stay," she said with tears streaming down her face. "I thought I was healed from all the trauma from my abuse, but my skin is crawling. Your story stirred up stuff in me, and I am not okay."

I could relate to this woman. I had been there a million times before. The feeling that you are not okay, and all you want to do is run. Satan doesn't want us to walk in healing. He wants us to run and continue to live in our pain. It suddenly began to make sense. I knew why God had me stop speaking so unexpectedly. I stopped so that several of us could minister and pray specifically over that sister in Christ at that particular time. After praying, we let her know that it was okay if she had to leave. There would be no judgment, but we also shared how the enemy uses situations to prevent the healing God wants to provide for her. We encouraged her to keep pressing into the Lord. The next day, she returned—praise the Lord!

On day two of the retreat, I talked about my abortion, trauma, and forgiveness. I shared my surrendering of hate and bitterness and forgiving those who hurt me. I testified how by surrendering everything at the foot of the cross, God set me free, and at that moment, the chains began to fall off of me. When I finished sharing, I encouraged the women to pray and ask God if they needed forgiveness or if they needed to forgive someone else. I then felt like the Lord wanted to allow the women to come up to the microphone and share what was on their hearts. One by one, they started to come up, and each woman bravely shared her painful story and laid it at the cross. It was beautiful to see women who had been sitting in the church hurting for years finally lay down that pain, exchange it for freedom, and begin the healing process.

That women's retreat was a beautiful testimony of what God can do when we

ONE BY ONE, THEY STARTED TO COME UP, AND EACH WOMAN BRAVELY SHARED HER PAINFUL STORY AND LAID IT AT THE CROSS.

lay down our pain and exchange it for the freedom and peace that only Christ can bring. After many of the women shared their stories, they came up to me and said, "I have never told anyone till today." So many of them sat in silence and shame. That retreat helped them to understand they were not alone. Many of them had no idea that there were others, attending the same church, who shared their same secret. Some were friends and even attended the same Bible study together. But this church retreat was a wonderful time of healing. The church allowed the women to share the deep hurts from their past, seek forgiveness, and forgive themselves or others. We ended the retreat praising and worshiping our hearts out to Jesus.

I refer to that weekend as my first She Found His Grace conference, marking the beginning of my ministry by that name. Northside Baptist Church graciously allowed me to share my abortion testimony. Abortion should be talked about in the church. Many women and men sitting in church are not walking in freedom from their past abortions. I know; I was one of them. But the church needs to understand that abortion hurts not only women but men, grandfathers, grandmothers, siblings, and the whole family. If not addressed, abortion will lead to more breakdown in the family. On any given Sunday, a dad is grieving over a past abortion and feeling unworthy of being a father to his family. Every year, women are dreading Mother's Day celebrations because of regret and shame. I believe one of the crucial things a church can do is acknowledge post-abortive mothers and fathers, and pray for us and remind us of God's love and forgiveness.

It has been a blessing to connect online with women from all over the world and share my story of healing. She Found His Grace gets messages all the time from women who are thinking of aborting their child. It is always my goal to connect them to someone in their hometown. But our ministry cannot do this alone. Pregnancy centers cannot do this alone. We need people in the church willing to roll up their sleeves to embrace life alongside single mothers or a teenage couple with an unplanned pregnancy. We need families like the Taylors, who took me in as a young teenage mom, gave me a safe place to live, and loved me well. We need people who will not only walk with women during their pregnancy but become life-long friends.

There is a great ministry opportunity that many churches are not embracing because we have allowed abortion to become a political issue instead of a discipleship issue. We can argue over abortion laws, but if Jesus Christ does not transform a person's heart, then abortion will continue. If the church remains silent over this crucial topic, then post-abortive mothers and fathers will continue to sit inside the walls of their churches, hurting and broken. In remaining silent, the church will continue to see problems with addiction, broken families, and people not fully walking in the freedom of Christ. The church has everything to gain by offering abortion ministry and everything to lose by not.

FINDING GOD'S GRACE

To make abortion unthinkable is to disciple individuals and allow God to transform their hearts and minds. Discipleship brought me healing. I am grateful for all those who pointed me in the right direction. The night I called out to God from my pit, God not only rescued me, but he transformed my life. I am a new creation because of the saving power of Jesus Christ. He brought healing and freedom to all my broken pieces. I am walking in the wholeness of Jesus Christ, and all I want is for others to find it as well.

Anyone who reads my story will see that I am not good. I am desperately in need of the Savior. But what I hope people take away from my story is that Christ, my Savior, is good. The Bible says, "But God demonstrates his own love for us in this: While we were still sinners, Christ died for us" (Romans 5:8). He loves me, and I was never beyond his reach. No one is beyond his reach. Not the mother or father who aborted, not the drug addict or alcoholic, not even the abuser or rapist.

But as I come to the end of my story here, I leave with one of the hardest parts to share. I would love to be able to testify that the relationships with my parents and my sister have been restored. That has been my prayer for years. A long time ago, abortion wounded my whole family. That day at the abortion clinic changed all of us. The hurt ran deep. It pulled us apart in a million different directions. It didn't affect just me; it affected all those close to me. My heart's desire is for the Lord to restore all of what the trauma in my family destroyed. That hasn't happened yet, but I haven't given up hope.

> WE ALL HAVE BROKEN PIECES, BUT JESUS IS REALLY GOOD AT PUTTING THEM BACK TOGETHER. THAT'S GREAT NEWS.

I would not be honest if I said I never struggled with my family not being complete. I have always wanted my family to have normal relationships. I miss not having family holidays with them, celebrating birthdays together, or just talking with them on the phone. Even though I am blessed with Bruce's family, and our kids and their families, not spending time with my family hurts. But faith is allowing God to mold me to love even when it hurts.

One day I was struggling with all the hurt over my parents. With tears streaming down my face, I began praying about this rejection from my family. I started searching Scripture, and the Lord led me to Psalm 27:10: "Though my father and mother forsake me, the LORD will receive me." Once again, God put his healing balm on my heart. I was already received. God had me in the palm of his hands throughout my life, even in some of my darkest moments. It wasn't that my parents didn't want or love me, but they were hurting and needed deep healing.

I wish I could end my book saying that my family story is redeemed, but it has not happened yet. The great news is, this story is not over yet; God is still writing it. So I pray for them. And on the hard days of my heart hurting, I turn to God's truth. I cling to his Word and pray that they feel his love even more on those days, that they would have their own radical encounter. My heart's desire is to have them experience the same lavish love I did. I want them to experience the same healing balm on their hearts and have the chains fall off of them so they can walk in freedom. We all have broken pieces, but Jesus is really good at putting them back together. That's great news.

One thing is for sure; my family has heard stories about Jesus. I listened to those same stories as a young girl when Mr. Whistler introduced me to Jesus Christ and the Bible. But I didn't really understand. It is my prayer that they will come to know and truly understand the love of Jesus Christ. My heart aches for it, and I just have to keep placing them at the feet of Christ. I'm not responsible for trying to put my family back together. I am trusting God that he is still working all things out for good according to his purpose (Romans 8:28). I have learned to see my family as people who are lost, who need Jesus, and who have their own hurts. As much as I want to fix them, I can't. That is up to God to do, just like he did for me. I have to remind myself to get out of the way, pray, and not hinder the process.

Here's what I do know. None of us deserve salvation, healing, redemption, blessings, and all the other beautiful gifts that come from our heavenly Father. But that is what God's grace is—the unmerited favor of God. Finding God's grace is freedom. It's no longer being a slave to shame, guilt, depression, anger, or bitterness. It's being able to mourn the loss of my aborted baby, knowing I will see her in heaven one day. Finding his grace is seeing the beauty of God's blessings in my marriage, my children, their spouses, and the joyful laughter and smile of my precious granddaughter.

As I look at all the pieces of my life, I can honestly say God is good. He has been with me all along, and he was waiting for me to call out to him. God extended his hand and pulled me out of the pit. God's grace is the most beautiful gift you could ever accept, and he gives it freely to all those who ask.

Acknowledgments

First and foremost I want to thank my Savior: Jesus, you are everything to me. Without your grace redeeming me, I would not have a story to share of your lavish love, forgiveness, and healing.

To my loving husband, Bruce, who didn't bolt many times when you could have: Thanks for loving me at my worst and waiting for God to heal me and bring back my sparkle that was taken from me long ago. Thank you for your grace and for loving me well.

To my kids who bring me so much joy: I'm thankful that I can be your mom. God sure did bless me with two of the best. For so long, I did not feel like I deserved you, and yet God saw fit to call you mine. I'm proud of who you are. I love your heart for Jesus and am so thankful for your support as I have shared my story. I'm grateful that you showed grace and love to me many times when my actions did not deserve it.

To my son-in-law and daughter-in-law: We prayed for Cassie and Carter's future spouses ever since they were little. God answered our prayers through the two of you. You both have witnessed some ugly parts of our lives and have loved our family through all of it. This speaks volumes about who you are. Thank you for your grace, love, and support.

To my granddaughter: You are my sunshine and light up the world. It is my prayer that you, along with our future grandchildren, will grow up and change the world for Jesus and not let the world change you.

To the church that loved an unchurched pregnant teen-ager: You loved me so well. Thank you to all the churches that have demonstrated love to girls like me. To all the Chuck and Barbara Taylors, thank you for welcoming people into your home, for not being afraid to accept the broken and make them family. You impacted how I open my own home to others. Because of you, I don't see people as strangers but always someone we can make family.

To the Dyksen family: Thank you for loving me well, even when I wasn't lovable. Dad Dyksen, I will never forget you telling me not to ever leave again after being a runner. I can't even put into words how much that meant to me. Mom Dyksen, thank you for being a mom who taught me so much about how to manage a household and for showing me the love of many family dinners. Thank you for loving us, sup-porting us, and helping us to choose life.

To my children I've never met: After thirty-one years of never feeling like I could mourn the loss of Elliana Grace, I'm free to acknowledge you as a daughter whose life and purpose were cut way too short. I'm able to share your story to save other babies. My tribe finally feels complete. I can't wait to meet you and your brother, Malachi, in heaven. I'm so thankful for the sweet vision God gave me at my post-abortion retreat of both of you cheering me on. All four of my children support this book and are cheering me on. I can't put into words what that does to this mother's heart.

And lastly, thank you, Mr. Allen Whistler, for telling me about Jesus. When I was a little girl, you shared Psalm 119:105 in a Bible you gave me. Over and over again, God's Word has been a light on my path. Thank you for speaking life over me and planting the seed of *life* within me.

Notes

1. Amanda Gray, "Women's Pavilion to close March 18, ending 38 years of controversy," *South Bend Tribune*, March 12, 2016.

2. National Right to Life Mission Statement <nrlc.org/about/mission>.

3. St. Joseph County Circuit Court public record, Centerville, Michigan.

4. Ibid.

5. Ibid.

6. "Our Mission Statement," Right to Life Michiana <prolifemichiana.org/ourmission>.

7. Linda Cochrane, *Forgiven and Set Free: A Post-Abortion Bible Study for Women* (Grand Rapids, MI: Baker Books, 2015).

8. Find out more at prolifeaction.org.

9. Niki Kelly, "State yanks doctor's license," *The Journal Gazette*, August 26, 2016 <tinyurl.com/ycakyegn>.

10. Cathie Humbarger, Allen County Right to Life, comments given September 16, 2019 <tinyurl.com/y969rn2k>.

11. "Induced Abortion in the United States" Fact Sheet, Guttmacher Institute, September 2019 <tinyurl.com/l789emu>.

12. Lawrence B. Finer, et al., "Reasons U.S. Women Have Abortions: Quantitative and Qualitative Perspectives," *Perspectives on Sexual and Reproductive Health*, September 2005, 113 <tinyurl.com/y3kkwroj>.

13. "What is the Silent No More Awareness Campaign?"<silentnomoreawareness.org/about-us/index.aspx>.

She Found His Grace Ministry

Thank you for letting me share my story of hope and healing. If you have decided that now is the time for your healing journey, I want you to know that you are not alone. She Found His Grace Ministry looks forward to hearing from you. Please join our ministry family.

Website: serenadyksen.com
Instagram: she_found_his_grace
Twitter: shefoundhisgrace
Facebook: serenadyksen75 (speaker page)
Facebook: shefoundhisgrace (ministry page)

For speaking engagements and inquiries, email:
serenadyksenshefoundhisgrace@gmail.com

If you enjoyed this book, please consider leaving a review on Amazon, Goodreads, my Facebook pages, or my website.